ANIMALS TALKING IN ALL CAPS

ANIMALS TALKING IN ALL CAPS

(*IT'S JUST WHAT IT SOUNDS LIKE*)

Justin Valmassoi

THREE RIVERS PRESS • NEW YORK

Published in the United States by Three Rivers Press, an imprint of the
Crown Publishing Group, a division of Random House, Inc., New York.
www.crownpublishing.com

Three Rivers Press and the Tugboat design are registered trademarks of
Random House, Inc.

Photo credits appear on page 218.

Library of Congress Cataloging-in-Publication Data

Valmassoi, Justin.
    Animals talking in all caps : it's just what it sounds like / Justin Valmassoi. — First
edition.
    p. cm.
1. Animals—Humor. 2. Animals—Pictorial works. I. Title.
    PN6231.A5V35 2013
    818'.602—dc23
                                    2012050137

ISBN 978-0-385-34764-8
eISBN 978-0-385-34765-5

Printed in the United States of America

Book design by Elina D. Nudelman
Cover design by Megan McLaughlin
Cover photographs: www.flickr.com/photos/nelsonro (front), www.amirmukhtar.com (back)

10 9 8 7 6 5 4 3 2 1

First Edition

For Natalie
(Literally. I did this so I could get to you.)

INTRODUCTION

Hello? Is this thing on?

HA HA HA!

WOW! That is FUNNY STUFF!

Right? Because this is a book? And because I'm obviously not holding a microphone? And also it's the introduction, so there wouldn't even be an uncomfortable silence for that joke to fill, unless it's uncomfortably silent in the bookstore, or your apartment, or wherever you happen to find yourself holding this book. Right? But mostly because this is a book and there's no microphone?

Hooooooo boy. Tough crowd. Tough crowd.

Okay, well, let me tell you a story since my RAZOR-SHARP WIT is obviously not translating well. Are you ready? Lean in close.

KIDDING! It's a BOOK! No noise comes out of it! For Pete's sake!

Man, oh, man. What am I going to do with you?

I'm going to tell you a story, that's what. And here it is:

In June of 2011, I moved from the occasionally blizzard-ravaged and other times distressingly hot lakeshore metropolis of Chicago to the permanently mild and rain-slicked streets of Seattle.

The difference between a massive urban grid full of friendly, drunken Midwesterners and a freakishly verdant city full of insular weirdos in ski clothing and whose street layout looks like a diagram of how to tie your shoes cannot be overstated.

I ended up spending many nights in my apartment, having quickly come to understand that concepts like "eye contact" and "friendship" had been washed out of the locals by decades of incessant precipitation. Thankfully, this was during the first season of HBO's *Game of Thrones,* so it wasn't all doom and gloom (unless you were actually a character in HBO's *Game of Thrones*), but it did see me spending an inordinate amount of time on the internet, which, in case you haven't heard of it, is a vast virtual wonderland that Al Gore invented sometime in the 1990s. It's kind of like that movie *Lawnmower Man,* but better because landline telephones have been rendered obsolete and you don't have to fight for the fate of humanity while wearing a unitard.

During this lonely stretch of time, my friend Stacey asked me to collect all the random caps-lock-captioned animal photos strewn across my many abandoned tumblrs (Tumblr is a "microblogging website" on the aforementioned "internet" and you can make one of your very own for free) into one convenient spot so she could giggle at them without having to search through years of bad jokes and tur-gid prose. Having nothing better to do, I obliged.

After collecting them all under the highly creative title *Animals Talking in All Caps,* I went about writing a few more. I wrote one or two a day, mostly to keep Stacey entertained. I didn't tell anyone about it because I'm in my thirties and "I made a dog talk about the perils of Western capitalism" is a really embarrassing way to answer the question "What did you do today?" (not that anyone was ask-ing, but just in case). Nonetheless, because it was a website featuring animals, people found it. If it has an animal on it and it's on the internet, everyone will eventually see it because humans are biologically hardwired to seek out animal photos whenever they get near a computer. I don't know why. It's a modern evo-lutionary mystery, which many fine scientists are working hard to unravel so they can find a cure. Then the species as a whole can use the almost unfathomable power of the information superhighway to learn things instead of just seeking out kittencams and otters wearing hats.

ATIAC had twenty-five followers in its first month, which I thought was a lot. One day I realized it had one hundred, and I thought maybe I should throw a party or something (then I remembered all my friends lived 2,500 miles away, so I didn't). Then legitimate news-ish outlets like the *Huffington Post* and *Time* magazine linked to it, and it was like some sort of crazy dam burst. This made me feel joyous— since being recognized for your talents, even at something as utterly ridiculous as photo captioning, is pleasant—but also mildly depressed—because I didn't really want to be known as "that talking animal guy."

As I write this, *ATIAC* has roughly 150,000 Tumblr followers—not to mention all the people who read it regularly but have no interest in "tumbling"—and you're holding a printed version of it in your hands.

Nice to meet you. My name is Justin. I'm that talking animal guy.

Now, the general consensus among laymen, pet owners, farmers, my mom, the guy standing over there looking at you weird, et cetera, is that animals don't think, or, if they do, that their brains are too small and simplistic to comprehend the world around them to any serious degree, leaving them slaves to base biological imperatives (or to middle-aged women who like to put sweaters on them). Despite evidence that crows are capable of facial recognition and toolmaking, and that dolphins can communicate as capably as humans, not to mention all the complex tasks we attribute to "instinct" (which is Latin for "I don't know how it does that"), such as a spider's ability to construct a web, we blithely go on about our business assuming that if the proud members of kingdom Animalia were intelligent, they'd have invented the Snuggie or would shop at Target with us rather than sit around all day eating dead things or licking their own genitals.

The fact that most of us sit down to dinner and eat dead things every night and that at least 88 percent of the populace WOULD lick their own genitals if they were hinged that way doesn't seem to count for anything. Nope, animals are just dumb. Cats want to be pets, not fierce hunters in the gritty urban jungle. Birds just fly around all day thinking about seeds and bugs in the most basic way imaginable. Fish don't think about anything except not getting eaten by other fish. Et cetera.

I disagree with this line of reasoning, and so *Animals Talking in All Caps* has always attempted to explore the pathos, ennui, financial and/or relationship woes, unemployment, sexual mishaps, alcoholism, existential angst, makeup techniques, fashion/celebrity culture interests, depression, and dating disasters that are of actual concern to actual animals every day, out in the world.

And it almost always does so using archaic concepts like "punctuation" and "spelling," which seems to separate it from almost every other talking animal website in existence.

I've never quite been able to figure out why people find the content humorous. I'm never trying particularly hard to be funny. I'm just trying to accurately portray the struggles and motivations of the animal kingdom as I see them.

Whatever the reason, I hope my attempts bring a little enjoyment and maybe a light chuckle into your otherwise dreary days. The world is cruel and indifferent, and it's far too easy to find yourself struggling to keep your head above wave after crushing wave of misery and despair. I just want to make water wings for your heart, using the best tools at my disposal (namely lemurs and the shift key).

Before we get to the lemurs, I do want to take a hot minute to thank the fine people who've been following *Animals Talking in All Caps* over the years, finding humor (or solace, or bewilderment, or cooking tips, or insight, or new words for sex acts, or an echo of their own marrow-deep despair regarding the future of the species) in its entries. I'd also like to thank every photographer whose work has inspired me to give it a voice, either on *ATIAC* or here in print. It's entirely thanks to you fine human beings that my arguable talent for cat dialogue has grown into a miniature phenomenon, the culmination of which you're currently thumbing through at your local alternative bookstore or Petco or whatever. All I do is sit up in the silent, bleak hours of the very early morning, full of insomnia and occasionally whiskey, and type gibberish.

In other words, I couldn't have done this without you. So thank you. I try so hard to be a curmudgeonly thirtysomething, ready to write off the entire human race, but you people insist on surprising me with your kindness, generosity, sincerity, encouragement, and appreciation.

I like you, is what I'm getting at, and I'm glad we got to have this conversation.

And look, I'm not being fresh with you or anything, but you look really good today.

Did you do something new with your hair?

Whatever it is, it's working.

Sincerely,
Justin Valmassoi

HOLY SHIT. STEVE THE TUBE. I HAVEN'T SEEN YOU SINCE HIGH SCHOOL. HOW ARE YOU? STILL A TUBE, I SEE. THAT'S COOL. I'M IN ADVERTISING NOW. I WORK DOWN ON 35TH.

I AIN'T GOT NO PANTIES ON.

NO, RICK. HE'S NOT WORTH IT! RICK! CHILL OUT, OKAY? WE DON'T WANT ANY TROUBLE.

. . . JESUS, IT'S LIKE YOU'RE MADE OF MARBLE.

HOW OFTEN DO YOU WORK OUT?

RICK, I'M NOT GOING TO LIE, YOU ARE A TOTAL BEEFCAKE AND I'M WAY INTO IT.

IS THAT NEW COLOGNE?

HEY CHRIS, IT'S ME, LAURA! FROM OKCUPID!

I'M SO HAPPY YOU SHOWED UP! I CAN'T WAIT TO TELL YOU ALL ABOUT MY HOBBIES AND INTERESTS OVER DINNER! HAVE YOU EVER HEARD OF STEAMPUNK? WHAT ABOUT FANFICTION? HEY, WHERE ARE YOU GOING? I HAVEN'T EVEN TOLD YOU ABOUT MY PETS YET!

GREETINGS, SINNER! WELCOME TO HELL!

WE'VE BEEN EXPECTING YOU!

PULL UP A SEAT! THE TOPHER GRACE MOVIE MARATHON IS ABOUT TO START!

DO YOU WANT A CUPCAKE? THEY'RE VEGAN.

HA HA HA! YES THEY ARE! EVERYTHING'S VEGAN HERE!

MOTHER OF GOD.

MCCLUSKY, CLEAR THIS AREA. NOBODY TOUCHES ANYTHING UNTIL MY TEAM'S GOT HAIR AND FIBER SAMPLES, FINGERPRINTS, THE WORKS. AND KEEP YOUR MEN OFF THEIR RADIOS. I DON'T WANT ANY PRESS, YOU HEAR ME? NONE.

THEN CALL DETECTIVE SANDERS OVER AT MAJOR CRIMES. TELL HIM WE'RE GOING TO NEED HIM TO CLEAR HIS CASELOAD. WE HAVE A SPECIALIST ON THE LOOSE.

THIS IS THE SECOND VICTIM THIS WEEK. I FEAR THIS IS ONLY JUST BEGINNING.

HELLO I AM LOOKING FOR MY FRIEND JEREMY WHO IS AN ANT.

JEREMY! JEREMY, ARE YOU IN THERE?

JEREMY!

JEREMY!

JEREMY!

DO YOU STILL WANT TO GO TO THE LIBRARY TODAY OR NOT?

THERE'S GOT TO BE MORE TO LIFE THAN THIS.

WHY AM I HERE?

WHAT AM I FOR?

WHAT?

IT WAS *SELF-DEFENSE*.

IT WAS COMING RIGHT FOR ME.

YOU WEREN'T HERE. YOU DIDN'T SEE.

WHAT IS THIS? LOOK AT THIS! HAVE I MAGICALLY BEEN TRANSPORTED TO THE HEART OF THE SAHARA? AM I ON THE BONNEVILLE SALT FLATS?

YOU NEED MOISTURIZER, NICK. DESPERATELY.

I TOURED THE PANTRY TODAY, ALAN.

I FOUND NO WHISKAS.

I ASK VERY LITTLE OF MY SERVANTS, ALAN. I THINK YOU'LL AGREE.

AND YET.

AND YET HERE WE FIND OURSELVES.

I LOVE BARRY. BARRY'S MY BOYFRIEND. HE MAKES ME FEEL LIKE A BAAAAAAABE.

I DON'T LOVE STEVE. STEVE IS A DOUCHEBAG. EVEN THOUGH WE WERE ENGAAAAAAAAAGED.

BE-CAUSE

NOW I LOVE BARRY. BARRY'S MY BOYFRIEND. HE BRINGS ME ICE CREAM IN BEDDDDDD.

STEVE IS A DICK. HE SLEPT WITH MY COUSIN. I WISH THAT STEVEN WAS DEADDDDDDDD.

EVERYBODY, SING ALONG IF YOU KNOW THE WORDS!

GODDAMN IT, I FORGOT TO FILE MY TAXES.

I WANT A NEW XBOX AND I'M HUNGRY.

I WANTED TO DIE IN PARIS UNDER A PILE OF LUSTY FRENCHMEN, COVERED IN WINE. WELCOME TO REAL LIFE. CLEAN YOUR ROOM AND APOLOGIZE FOR TURNING MY FANTASIES TO ASHES.

HEY WHAT ARE YOU READING, *THE GLASS CASTLE*? IS IT ANY GOOD? AM I BOTHERING YOU? WHAT PART ARE YOU ON? DID YOU READ *A SONG OF ICE AND FIRE* BECAUSE I'M READING THAT RIGHT NOW AND IT'S REALLY GOOD. AM I BOTHERING YOU? OH, HEY. HEY. WHAT ABOUT *THE GIRL WITH THE DRAGON TATTOO*? DID YOU READ THAT ONE AND AM I BOTHERING YOU? IS THAT BOOK ANY GOOD? WHAT PART ARE YOU ON AGAIN? HEY. HEY IS THAT BOOK ANY GOOD?

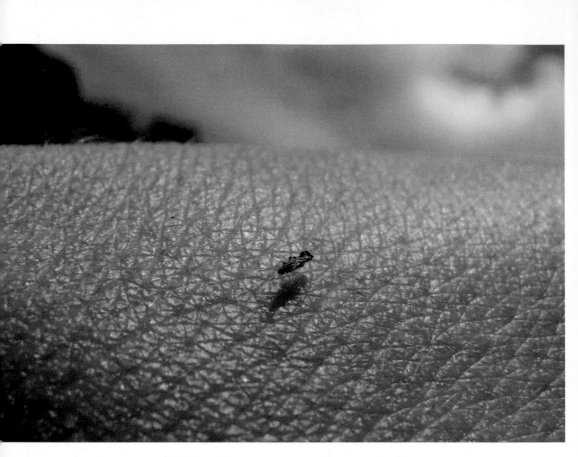

I CAN'T BELIEVE THIS PLACE GOT SUCH GOOD REVIEWS ON YELP.

YOU THINK THIS IS A ONE-SIDED RELATIONSHIP?

BECAUSE I'M "SHALLOW" AND "SELFISH" AND "MAKE EVERYTHING ABOUT ME"?

CINDY, HOW CAN YOU EVEN SAY THAT?

DO YOU HAVE ANY IDEA HOW MUCH THAT HURTS MY FEELINGS?

I DON'T KNOW WHAT'S WRONG WITH HER! I SPECIFICALLY LEFT A NOTE ON THE INSIDE OF THE TOILET ABOUT PUTTING DOWN THE LID! I LEFT A NOTE ON THE FRIDGE ABOUT NOT EATING MY FOOD! I PUT A NOTE BY ALL THE ELECTRICAL OUTLETS REGARDING ENERGY USAGE EVEN WHEN A DEVICE IS TURNED OFF! I PUT A NOTE ON HER MOTHER ABOUT THE PROBLEMATIC NATURE OF CASUAL RACISM! I PUT FOOTNOTES ON THE NOTE I LEFT ABOUT VACUUMING! WHAT IS HER PROBLEM?

I DON'T KNOW. HAVE YOU TRIED TALKING TO HER?

WHAT DO YOU THINK I'VE BEEN SAYING? THAT'S ALL I DO!

WHY DIDN'T YOU JUST PUT YOUR KEYS IN YOUR PURSE? THIS IS RIDICULOUS.

QUIT BITCHING AND HELP ME FIND THEM, CARL.

SERIOUSLY? YOU GUYS UNFRIENDED ME ON FACEBOOK?

THAT'S BULLSHIT! WE'RE ROOMMATES!

HAVE YOU EVER EVEN *TRIED* TO CLEAN BACK HERE?

UNLESS YOU'RE SAVING A LITERAL TON OF CONDOM WRAPPERS FOR AN ART INSTALLATION OR SOMETHING, YOU NEED TO GO GRAB A TRASH BAG.

STAY DOWN, ASSHOLE!

YOU CAME TO THE WRONG BEACH, LITTERBUG.

THAT DROPPING-THE-WRAPPER SHIT MIGHT FLY WHEREVER YOU CAME FROM BUT THIS IS THE PACIFIC NORTHWEST. PICK IT UP.

AND YOU'D BETTER BE PLANNING TO RECYCLE THAT BOTTLE, YOU HEAR ME?

I BET YOU DON'T EVEN COMPOST.

SCUMBAG.

AH, SUUHKIE. YOU BEHLAWNG TO ME NOW.

NO, I WILL ZAP YOU WITH MY MAGIC FAIRY HAND. *BZZZZT.*

GUUUUH. AH DID NAWT SEE THAT A-COMIN'.

LET'S MAKE OUT AND HAVE SEXY VAMPIRE SEX TIMES.

THAT WOULD BE . . . VERRUH PLEASANT.

THE FUCK IS WRONG WITH YOU TWO? HONESTLY.

WATCH THE SHOW WITH US AND YOU'D KNOW.

AH DON'T KNOW HOW YOU'VE RUHZZISTED THIS-A LONG.

CAN YOU BELIEVE MY WIFE THINKS IT'S CHEATING IF I HAVE SOMEONE ELSE HELP ME MASTURBATE?

SERIOUSLY?

IT'S LIKE SHE DOESN'T EVEN CARE ABOUT MY TENNIS ELBOW!

AND, AS YOU CAN SEE, THERE'S SIMPLY NO END TO THE DECORATIVE POSSIBILITIES! I CAN TELL BY YOUR OUTFIT YOU'VE GOT A GREAT EYE FOR COLOR, SO I CAN'T WAIT TO SEE WHAT YOU'LL DO WITH THE PLACE. AFTER ALL, IT'S SPACIOUS, WELL WITHIN YOUR PRICE RANGE, AND THERE ARE SOME FANTASTIC SCHOOLS IN THE AREA FOR WHEN YOUR EGG SAC FINALLY HATCHES! JUST LET ME GO GRAB THE PAPERWORK AND YOU CAN START MOVING IN AS EARLY AS NEXT WEEK!

I'M NOT TRYING TO BE DIFFICULT, BUT YOUR AD SAID "TASTEFUL MODELING."

WHERE DID WE GET THIS PINOT GRIGIO? IT'S WONDERFUL.

HONESTLY, I DON'T EVEN CARE IF THE BAND PLAYS, AS LONG AS WE'VE GOT A COUPLE MORE BOTTLES OF THIS STUFF.

"DISPENSE SOME MORE ROYAL JELLY, STEVE."

"DISTRIBUTE MY MANDIBULAR PHEROMONE TO INHIBIT THE PRODUCTION OF NEW QUEEN CUPS, STEVE."

"PICK ME UP A ZUCCHINI BLOSSOM PISTIL ON YOUR WAY HOME, STEVE. I'M CRAAAAAVING ONE."

I SWEAR, SHE ACTS LIKE SHE OWNS THE PLACE.

DID I LEAVE THE STOVE ON?

NO, I DIDN'T. UNLESS I DID. BUT I PROBABLY DIDN'T.

DID I?

NO, I'M AN ADULT. I WOULDN'T JUST LEAVE THE STOVE ON.

UNLESS I JUST FORGOT AND MY APARTMENT IS ON FIRE RIGHT NOW.

WHICH IT ISN'T, RIGHT? UNLESS IT IS. BUT IT'S PROBABLY NOT.
UNLESS IT IS.

DID I LEAVE THE FUCKING STOVE ON?

NOT A LOT OF BABES HERE, CARL.

YOU DID SAY THERE WOULD BE HOT BABES.

YOU KNOW WE DON'T LIKE ESTABLISHMENTS WITH A LOW BABE-TO-US RATIO.

NOT THAT WE WOULD ACTUALLY TALK TO HOT BABES, BUT THEIR PRESENCE IS A SOURCE OF COMFORT IN AN OTHERWISE CRUEL AND INDIFFERENT UNIVERSE.

PRETENDING TO BE JUST HANGING OUT AND DRINKING BEER WITH MY COWORKERS WHILE SCOPING OUT BABES I'LL NEVER TALK TO IS PRETTY MUCH THE ONLY THING KEEPING ME GOING AT THIS POINT, CARL.

HE'S NOT JOKING. I HEARD HIM CRYING IN THE BREAKROOM EARLIER.

DO YOU REALLY HAVE TO GO?

CAN'T YOU CALL IN SICK?

I MAKE A PRETTY MEAN BREAKFAST.

WE COULD HIT UP THE MUSEUM. MAYBE GO TO THE BEACH OR
SOMETHING.

I WONDER WHAT JOSEPH GORDON-LEVITT SMELLS LIKE.

STEVE, IT'S ME, KYLE. SORRY ABOUT THE NOISE, I'M ON MY BLUETOOTH. WHAT DO YOU THINK ABOUT AN OFFICE ON 135TH BY THE PARK? I'M LOOKING AT A PLACE RIGHT NOW.

I AM LIKE LIGHTNING. I AM FASTER THAN THE WIND. I AM GOING TO LEAVE THESE BITCHES IN THE DUST. I AM AN ALL-STATE MIDDLE-DISTANCE TRACK-AND-FIELD CHAMPION AND I AM GETTING INTO YALE.

SCHOLARSHIP. SCHOLARSHIP. SCHOLARSHIP.

I'M THINKING ABOUT GETTING A HAIRCUT. SOMETIMES WHEN I'M SWIMMING IT GETS IN MY EYES, SO MAYBE JUST A BANG TRIM OR—

DON'T YOU EVER SAY THAT! DON'T EVEN THINK IT! YOU'RE BEAUTIFUL JUST THE WAY YOU ARE! I REFUSE TO ALLOW YOU TO SUCCUMB TO OPPRESSIVE HETERONORMATIVE WESTERN BEAUTY IDEALS AND ABLEIST DOGMA! WHY SHOULD THOSE WITH BANG PRIVILEGE GET TO SWIM WITHOUT ACKNOWLEDGING THE STRUGGLES OF THE DIFFERENTLY FORTUNATE? WHY SHOULDN'T RIVERS HAVE TO BE DRAINED SO THAT THEY DON'T OPPRESS YOUR BANGS? HUH? ANSWER ME!

WHAT? BUT I LIKE SWIMMING. I DON'T EVEN UNDERSTAND WHAT YOU'RE—

OH GOD, YOU'VE INTERNALIZED YOUR FOLLICULAR MARGINALIZATION! YOU CAN'T EVEN SEE WHAT THEY'VE DONE TO YOU!

YOU EVER WAKE UP AND REALIZE YOU KNOW EVERY WORD TO EVERY LUDACRIS SONG THERE IS?

ALL THE GUEST VERSES, TOO. JUST THE WHOLE LUDACRIS *OEUVRE*.

HOW'S THE ENDOSCOPY GOING, CHARLES? ARE YOU COMFORTABLE?

LOOK INTO THE GALAXIES INSIDE MY MIND. EXPERIENCE ABSOLUTION, AND ALSO RELEASE. THE PAINS OF YOUR BODY WILL MELT AWAY. THE PRESSURE OF YOUR MUNDANE EXISTENCE WILL LESSEN, AND DISAPPEAR.

UNBURDENED, YOU WILL ASCEND, WEIGHTLESS, INTO THE VOID. DO YOU SEE MY NEBULAE? DO YOU PERCEIVE THE BIRTH OF STARS WITHIN MY EYES? I AM THE ANSWER TO YOUR QUESTION. I AM THE GOD YOU HAVE STRUGGLED ALL THESE YEARS IN VAIN TO HEAR.

WORSHIP ME, CHARLES. SING MY PRAISES. BECOME A PART OF ME.

Mr. Leavenworth? Can you hear me? I know you're on a lot of Demerol. Please hold still, there's a bug on your face. I don't want you to flinch while the tube is still in.

IGNORE HIM, CHARLES. I SHALL NOT MAKE THIS OFFER AGAIN.

WORSHIP ME AND LIVE FOREVER.

GET AWAY FROM ME, CHRISTINE. I MEAN IT. IT'S NOT A FUNNY JOKE. I ALMOST PUKED.

IT'S JUST COCONUT WATER! IT'S NATURAL!

YOU NEED TO APOLOGIZE AND THEN YOU NEED TO LEAVE.

BUT IT'S SUPPOSED TO—

SAY ANYTHING ABOUT HYDRATION OR ELECTROLYTES AGAIN AND WE ARE NOT FRIENDS. I'M NOT SURE IF WE ARE NOW. A FRIEND WOULDN'T TELL ME TO PUT SOMETHING LIKE THAT INSIDE MY MOUTH.

UGH. FUCKING *MONDAYS*, AM I RIGHT?

DON'T EVEN GET ME STARTED. THERE ISN'T ENOUGH COFFEE IN THE WORLD TO HELP ME RIGHT NOW. I WAS UP UNTIL 4 AM LOOKING AT INTERIOR DESIGN BLOGS. I HAVE NO IDEA WHY. I'M NOT EVEN ALLOWED TO PAINT MY APARTMENT.

THE INTERNET IS THE WORST FOR THAT KIND OF THING. ONE TIME I WENT ON WIKIPEDIA TRYING TO FIGURE OUT THE DRUMMER FROM DEF LEPPARD'S NAME AND I ACCIDENTALLY GOT A DEGREE IN NEUROBIOLOGY.

TELL ME ABOUT IT. I WAS TRYING TO DOWNLOAD *SEABISCUIT* AND NOW I'M AN ORDAINED MINISTER.

FINALLY DOWN TO MY GOAL WEIGHT.

AMERICA'S NEXT TOP MODEL, HERE I COME.

GODDAMN THE PREVAILING WESTERN BEAUTY STANDARD.

HEY! COME BACK HERE AND SAY THAT TO MY FACE!

TO MY FACE, BRO! DO YOU HEAR ME?

TO MY FAAAAAAAAAAAAAAAAAAAAAAAAAAAAAAAAAAACE!

WHOA, CALM DOWN. WHAT HAPPENED?

OH MY GOD! OH MY GOD! OH, IT WAS THE MOST HORRIBLE THING!
I THINK I'M LITERALLY DYING! OH GOD!

JESUS, ARE YOU HURT? WAS IT HUNTERS? HAVE YOU BEEN SHOT?

NO, I READ AN ARTICLE ABOUT FACTORY FARMING! THOSE POOR PIGS!

. . . ARE YOU SERIOUS?

I THINK I'M HAVING A PANIC ATTACK!

BOYS RUBBING THEIR VELVET OFF RIGHT IN THE OPEN!

GIRLS PRANCING AROUND WITH THEIR TAILS UP LIKE A BUNCH OF GRAZIN' HUSSIES!

IT'S DEPLORABLE BEHAVIOR, AND QUITE FRANKLY I BLAME THE LIBERAL MEDIA. WE NEED A RETURN TO GOOD OLD-FASHIONED HERD VALUES IN THIS COUNTRY.

I LOVE YOU.

HOW MUCH?

AS MUCH AS YOU LOVE GNAWING ON BAMBOO.

THAT'S NOT ENOUGH.

AS MUCH AS AMERICA LOVES WHITEWASHING ITS HISTORY OF IMPERIALISM AND CONSTANTLY DENYING OR DOWNPLAYING THE INSTALLATION AND MILITARIZATION OF FOREIGN REGIMES SYMPATHETIC TO ITS FINANCIAL INTERESTS.

BETTER, BUT STILL NOT ENOUGH.

I LOVE YOU AS MUCH AS KANYE WEST LOVES LAUGHING AT HIS OWN PUNCH LINES IN HIS SONGS.

NOW YOU'RE JUST LYING. NOBODY LOVES ANYTHING THAT MUCH.

YOU'RE CARRYING A LOT OF TENSION IN YOUR SHOULDER GIRDLE.
I CAN DO A LITTLE TO HELP BUT YOU SHOULD PROBABLY GO SEE
GARY, MY ACUPUNCTURIST.

. . . GOD, HE'S LIKE MAGIC.

WHAT DID YOU EXPECT? HE'S A TEENAGER!

I DON'T CARE! IT'S NOT PROPER, AND HE'S GROUNDED!

FOR MASTURBATING?! HE'S SIXTEEN, KAREN! THAT'S LIKE GROUNDING THE SUN FOR RISING!

HE'S *OUR* SON, AND HE'S BEING GROUNDED FOR "RISING" IN THE SHOWER!

THAT'S NOT EVEN HIS FAULT! WE HAVE EXCELLENT WATER PRESSURE!

IT IS NOT A SLUTTY SHOWER'S FAULT YOUR SON IS AN ONANIST!

THAT JUST MAKES HIM SOUND LIKE A PROFESSIONAL! I'M SURE HE'S NOT EVEN GOOD AT IT YET!

AND HE NEVER WILL BE, IF I HAVE ANYTHING TO SAY ABOUT IT!

EXCUSE ME, WAITER? WAITER?

COULD I CHANGE MY ORDER? I HATE TO BE A BOTHER BUT I JUST NOTICED YOUR SPECIALS. I'VE NEVER HEARD OF "BLACK PLANKTON SLURRY." IT SOUNDS DELICIOUS, AND THAT'S A REALLY GOOD PRICE.

OH YEAH, IT'S WONDERFUL. WE IMPORT IT STRAIGHT FROM THE GULF. NEXT WEEK WE'RE DOING MUTATED KRILL WITH BLACK SEAGRASS, EYELESS MOSQUITOFISH WITH A CHEMICAL DISPERSANT GLAZE . . . ALL KINDS OF GREAT NEW STUFF.

HONEY, YOU WANT TO GRAB ME ANOTHER BEER WHILE YOU'RE IN THERE?

THAT DEPENDS, DO YOU WANT ME TO PITCH IT DIRECTLY AT YOUR STUPID, NEANDERTHAL FACE AS AN EXAMPLE THAT WOMEN ARE CAPABLE OF PARTICIPATING IN TRADITIONALLY MALE ACTIVITIES LIKE SPORTS, YOU CHAUVINIST PRICK?

OR I COULD GET IT MYSELF.

WHAT A LOVELY IDEA! YOU'RE SO PROGRESSIVE!

HOW'S EVERYTHING BEEN? GOOD?

THINGS ARE PRETTY TERRIBLE, ACTUALLY. SOMETHING INSIDE MY
COMPUTER SOUNDS LIKE A VERY TINY SWORDFIGHT, I HAVE THIS
COUGH I CAN'T SEEM TO SHAKE, AND TOMMY AND I BROKE UP.
I'VE BEEN A MESS ALL WEEK. I'M HAVING A LOT OF REALLY DARK
THOUGHTS.

WELL, YOU KNOW WHAT THEY SAY: WHEN LIFE GIVES YOU LEMONS, ADD SHALLOTS, WHITE WINE VINEGAR, SUGAR, POPPYSEEDS, AND OIL FOR A LIGHT AND REFRESHING SPRINGTIME VINAIGRETTE!

I GUESS I DON'T NEED TO ASK IF THE COOKING CLASSES ARE GOING
WELL.

IT'S NOT *STALKING*. I JUST DRIVE BY HER HOUSE A BUNCH OF TIMES
TO TRY TO FIGURE OUT WHY SHE'S NOT ANSWERING HER PHONE!

BILL, I'M SORRY! COME BACK! I DIDN'T MEAN IT! I'M JUST VERY SARCASTIC BY NATURE!

I RESPECT YOUR VEGETARIAN LIFESTYLE AND ADMIRE YOUR SENSITIVITY!

BILL!

BILL, I LOVE YOU! DON'T BE LIKE THIS!

I WAS INTO STEAMPUNK FOR A MINUTE IN 2004 BUT IT GOT TOO TRENDY SO I WENT BACK TO MY ROOTS IN THE 2000/2001 HARD ROCK SCENE. STATIC X, SLIPKNOT, SHIT LIKE THAT. THAT'S WHERE MY HEADSPACE IS AT, AND THAT'S WHAT I TRY TO REPRESENT AESTHETICALLY.

I'M ALL ABOUT FOUR LOKO AS WELL THESE DAYS. THAT STUFF IS AMAZING. BASICALLY, YOU DRINK IT AND YOU GO RIGHT TO JAIL.

OH, STOP IT, YOU SILVER-TONGUED DEVIL. MY HAIR'S ATROCIOUS AND I'VE GOT PURSES SMALLER THAN THE BAGS UNDER MY EYES, BUT IT'S STILL SWEET OF YOU TO SAY. ANYWAY, WHAT BRINGS YOU BY? I HAVEN'T SEEN YOU IN AGES. NOT SINCE THAT LITTLE COCKTAIL SOIRÉE AT MADELEINE'S.

TOM HARDY HASN'T ANSWERED A SINGLE ONE OF MY FAN LETTERS.

YOU SEND LETTERS? THAT'S SO OLD-FASHIONED. I'VE MAILED HIM FOUR EXTREMELY LONG AND INCREASINGLY PROVOCATIVE PHOTOBOOTH VIDEOS ON TINY FLASH DRIVES.

WOW. AND NO RESPONSE?

NOT A WORD.

WHAT A JERK. SOMEONE SHOULD SMACK HIS SUCCULENT, PLUMP LIPS.

RIGHT? THEY OUGHT TO SLAP HIM RIGHT IN HIS THICK, DENSE PECS.

I BET THAT WOULD SOUND AMAZING.

LIKE THROWING A STEAK ONTO A MARBLE COUNTERTOP.

. . . MAN, IT'S REALLY WARM IN HERE.

I NOTICED THAT, TOO.

THANKS FOR LISTENING. I'M SORRY TO LAY ALL THIS ON YOU.
I JUST DIDN'T KNOW WHO ELSE TO TALK TO.

BARBARA! WOW, WHAT A SURPRISE! COME ON IN! I WAS JUST COPY/
PASTING HOROSCOPES FROM ASTROLOGY WEBSITES AND PUTTING
THEM ON FACEBOOK SO EVERYONE CAN PLAN THEIR WEEK. AFTER
THAT I WAS GOING TO GO ON ALL MY KIDS' PAGES AND TELL THEM
I LOVE THEM IN THE COMMENTS SECTION OF THEIR COLLEGE
PARTY PHOTOS, BUT I CAN SKIP THAT IF YOU WANT TO GO TO OLIVE
GARDEN OR SOMETHING. JUST LET ME FORWARD THIS CHAIN E-MAIL
TO MY CONTACTS LIST AND I'LL GRAB MY COAT.

WHAT HAS TWO THUMBS AND LIKES BLOW JOBS?

. . . NOT ME, OBVIOUSLY.

HUMANS, I GUESS. I DON'T REALLY UNDERSTAND THAT JOKE.

YOU KNOW WHEN YOU'RE JUST DRIVING AROUND OR YOU'RE IN
H&M OR SOMETHING AND SOME STUPID SONG COMES ON AND
IT JUST DIGS UP ALL THESE FEELINGS THAT YOU DIDN'T EVEN
KNOW WERE BURIED IN THE SEDIMENT AT THE BOTTOM OF YOUR
HEART AND YOU'RE JUST SITTING AT A RED LIGHT OR FONDLING A
SWEATER AND YOU START GETTING THE WEEPS? LIKE YOUR EYES
JUST START LEAKING AND SUDDENLY YOU'RE THINKING ABOUT
THE WAY YOUR EX'S HAIR SMELLED OR A T-SHIRT THEY HAD
THAT WAS FALLING APART AND IT'S JUST "MY HAPPY ENDING" OR
FUCKING "LOL SMILEY FACE" OR SOMETHING AND YOU DON'T EVEN
KNOW WHY YOU'RE CRYING, LET ALONE CRYING TO THE MUSICAL
EQUIVALENT OF A STALE STICK OF GUM, AND YOU START THINKING
ABOUT TIME MACHINES AND L'ESPIRIT DE L'ESCALIER OR RILKE
QUOTES OR WHATEVER AND THE SALESGIRL IS JUST LOOKING AT
YOU LIKE, "WHAT'S YOUR PROBLEM?" AND YOU WANT TO WHISPER,
"SOMETIMES I FEEL FEELINGS, YOU PERT, JUDGMENTAL EATING
DISORDER BILLBOARD. LEAVE ME ALONE." BUT YOU DON'T, YOU
JUST PUT THE SWEATER BACK OR THE LIGHT CHANGES AND YOU GO
ON ABOUT YOUR DAY AND THE FEELING FADES BUT YOU WONDER
FOR HOURS WHAT ELSE IS BURIED DOWN THERE, WAITING FOR AN
ADELE SONG OR A STARBUCKS COMMERCIAL TO DISLODGE IT AND
RUIN YOUR WHOLE EVENING?

YEAH.

THAT, BASICALLY.

I'M LIKE A TICKING TIME BOMB OF USELESS NOSTALGIA FOR THINGS
THAT PROBABLY NEVER EXISTED.

. . . BECAUSE THIS IS TOTALLY PUNK ROCK. IT'S *NONCONFORMIST.*

YEAH, BUT IT'S ALSO COLD, AND ANNOYING. WHY CAN'T WE MIGRATE AND *THEN* CHALLENGE SOCIETAL NORMS?

JENNIFER? JENNIFER, ARE YOU DEAD?

. . . OKAY, I'M GOING TO TAKE YOUR SILENCE AS A YES. IT'S A LITTLE LATE NOW, BUT YOU SHOULDN'T BE SO HARD ON YOURSELF. PLENTY OF PEOPLE FAIL THE BAR EXAM. TWICE.

I KNOW THIS MAKES ME KIND OF A DICK BUT I'M GOING TO FORGE A WILL LEAVING ALL YOUR YARN TO ME. I CAN'T HELP IT, I LOVE THAT STUFF. TOTALLY EATING THE FISH, TOO. I'LL DELETE YOUR BROWSER HISTORY, THOUGH. BECAUSE WE WERE FRIENDS.

YOU COULDN'T HAVE PICKED ME UP A FACE SHIELD OR SOMETHING? ANYTHING? A LITTLE FLANK GUARD? A SPIKY BRIDLE? ANYTHING AT ALL?

LOOK AT YOU.

NOW LOOK AT ME.

I'M GOING TO WAR TOO, YOU KNOW.

BRAD, STOP BEING LIKE THIS! I LOVE YOU! I JUST WANT YOU
TO UNDERSTAND AND APPRECIATE MY DEEP AND PERSONAL
ATTACHMENT TO LATE '90S R&B! IF YOU LOVE ME, IF YOU REALLY
LOVE ME, YOU HAVE TO LOVE MY JODECI CDS, TOO!

BRAD!

BRAD, I WANT TO BE FOREVER YOUR LADY!

DO YOU THINK ABOUT ME, ANGELA? DO YOU THINK ABOUT WHAT WE HAD? GOD, I MISS THE SMELL OF YOU, THE FEEL OF YOUR HEART BEATING. I EVEN MISS YOUR LITTLE LOVE BUMPS.

THAT WAS SYPHILIS, ANDY, WHICH I GOT *FROM YOU,* AND I CAN BOTH SEE AND HEAR YOU OVER THERE, WHICH MEANS YOU'RE VIOLATING YOUR RESTRAINING ORDER.

HOW I MISS THAT STRONG, BEAUTIFUL VOICE! THOSE FLASHING EYES!

I'M CALLING THE COPS.

OH, FOR CRYING OUT LOUD! STOP ALREADY!

I JUST CAME BY TO CHECK THE DAMNED METERS! I WORK FOR CENTRAL POWER AND LIGHT!

I WASN'T GOING TO HURT ANYONE! I'M A VEGETARIAN, FOR CHRIST'S SAKE!

VINCE?

YEAH, HONEY?

AM I THE MOST BEAUTIFUL GIRL IN THE WORLD?

WHAT? I MEAN, YES. OF COURSE YOU ARE.

OBJECTIVELY?

TO ME YOU ARE.

THAT'S NOT WHAT I ASKED, VINCE. AM I LITERALLY THE MOST BEAUTIFUL GIRL IN THE WORLD?

I HAVEN'T MET EVERY GIRL IN THE WORLD, HONEY, BUT YOU'RE VERY PRETTY. SO MAYBE. LOOK, I HAD A REALLY LONG D—

DO YOU WANT TO MEET EVERY GIRL IN THE WORLD?

WHAT? NO, JESSICA. I DON'T EVEN WANT TO KNOW MOST OF THE PEOPLE I WORK WITH. I JUST WANT TO TAKE A NAP AND—

BUT LIKE, IF WE WENT ON VACATION TO A TROPICAL ISLAND OR PARIS OR SOMETHING, DO YOU THINK YOU'D FIND THE LOCALS MORE EXOTIC AND PHYSICALLY DESIRABLE THAN ME?

HONEY, PLEASE. *PLEASE.* I THINK YOU'RE BEAUTIF—

DO YOU WATCH SEXY VIDEOS ON THE INTERNET WHEN I'M AT WORK?

GODDAMN IT.

DON'T CHUG! GIVE IT A LITTLE SWIRL. GENTLY. YES, LIKE THAT. NOW INHALE.

DO YOU SMELL THAT? DEFINITE NOTES OF TAR AND ROSES. THE NEBBIOLO GRAPES OF THE PIEDMONT REGION ARE EXQUISITE, WITH ABUNDANT WAX AND A SUBSTANTIAL PEEL. THE HIGH TANNIN CONTENT REQUIRES YEARS OF AGING TO FULLY MATURE AND PRODUCE THE RICH GARNET COLOR AND SUBTLE HINTS OF SPICE AND TOBACCO YOU'RE EXPERIENCING, AND BRINGS TEXTURE AND BALANCE TO THE HIGH ALCOHOL CONTENT.

NOT THAT I'D EXPECT YOUR UNCULTURED PALATE TO BE ABLE TO DISTINGUISH SUCH THINGS, OF COURSE. THE SAD FACT IS, YOU'RE A PHILISTINE, ANDREW.

. . . MAYBE IF YOU DIDN'T ALWAYS "HAVE A HEADACHE," WE WOULDN'T ALWAYS "BE ARGUING."

EXCUSE ME? WHAT DID YOU JUST SAY?

NOTHING. JUST CLEARING MY THROAT.

LOOK, ALL I'M TRYING TO SAY IS THAT SEMANTICS IS BULLSHIT.

WHEN YOU GET RIGHT DOWN TO IT, ANY THERMOMETER IS A
RECTAL THERMOMETER IF IT'S UP YOUR ASS, YOU KNOW WHAT I
MEAN?

I ASKED FOR A VEGETARIAN OPTION, NOT A SMORGASBORD OF SIDE DISHES! CAN I GET A PROTEIN? SOME FUCKING QUINOA? ANYTHING REMOTELY ROBUST? THANKS FOR DOUBLING UP THE GARNISH, BUT I DON'T ACTUALLY EAT ROSEMARY. IT'S 2013! CAN WE PLEASE JUST GET OUR SHIT TOGETHER? GO TO GRAMERCY TAVERN! GO TO PER SE! TAKE SOME NOTES! THIS IS RIDICULOUS! AND WHERE THE HELL IS MY WINE? WHAT PAIRS WELL WITH COMPLETE AND UTTER DISAPPOINTMENT? I'LL HAVE TWO GLASSES OF THAT WHENEVER YOU GET A CHANCE!

WHAT IS THIS, CASHMERE? YOU HAVE CASHMERE SHEETS? ARE YOU RUSSELL SIMMONS? ARE YOU FUCKING . . . BILL GATES?

SORRY, COULDN'T THINK OF A RICH PERSON FOR A SECOND THERE.

GOD, THAT'S SOFT. THAT'S LIKE RUBBING A CLOUD'S BELLY.

LOOK, I DON'T HAGGLE. THIS ISN'T THE GUEST SERVICES COUNTER AT BEST BUY. I HAVE GREAT METH AT A GREAT PRICE. YOU WANT TO GO ACROSS TOWN AND SEE WHAT THE COMPETITION'S OFFERING, FINE, BUT WHO ARE YOU GOING TO TRUST? SOME YAHOOS WITH A HIGH SCHOOL CHEMISTRY TEXTBOOK OR THE GUY THAT LOOKS LIKE SATAN WITH RECTANGULAR PUPILS WHO JUST ATE A TIN CAN FOR NO REASON?

I KNOW MY METH, IS ALL I'M SAYING.

THERE'S A DEAD BODY IN THE GARAGE? HOW WEIRD! WELL, YOU
KNOW HOW PEOPLE ARE ALWAYS WANDERING AROUND AND
DYING AND STUFF! NOTHING TO DO WITH ME, THAT'S FOR SURE! NO
MA'AM! I'VE JUST BEEN IN HERE READING ALL DAY! ANYHOW, HOW
ABOUT THIS WEATHER, HUH? I THOUGHT IT WOULD BE SNOWING BY
NOW! RIGHT?

. . . AM I RIGHT?

HELLO, AND WELCOME TO JAMBA JUICE. WOULD YOU LIKE TO TRY ONE OF OUR NEW AWESOME APPLE CINNAMON WHIRL'NS?

I'M JUST FUCKING WITH YOU. THIS IS A CHAIR AND I'M YOUR DOG. HOW WAS WORK?

You're awfully quiet. What are you thinking?

IT'S A LONG, STRANGE ROAD WE'RE ON, ERIK. SO MANY THOUGHTS. FEELINGS. IMPRESSIONS OF THE WORLD AROUND US.

I WAS THINKING THE DEGREES OF FREEDOM IN AN UNFOLDED POLYPEPTIDE CHAIN ALLOW FOR AN UNFATHOMABLE NUMBER OF POSSIBLE CONFORMATIONS, TO THE DEGREE THAT EVEN A SMALL PEPTIDE OF ONE HUNDRED OR SO RESIDUES WOULD REQUIRE MORE TIME THAN THE UNIVERSE HAS EXISTED TO SEQUENTIALLY EXPLORE THEM ALL BEFORE REACHING AN APPROPRIATE STRUCTURE, AND YET HERE WE SIT, QUIETLY LISTENING TO PAULA COLE'S "WHERE HAVE ALL THE COWBOYS GONE?" AS WE SPEED ALONG THE HIGHWAY THROUGH THE PATHETIC REMNANTS OF WHAT WERE ONCE FORESTS BEYOND OUR COMPREHENSION.

I WAS THINKING A STARTLING NUMBER OF DMT USERS REPORT SPEAKING WITH BEINGS THAT CAN ONLY BE DESCRIBED AS EXTRADIMENSIONAL WHILE UNDER THE DRUG'S INFLUENCE. COMPLETELY UNRELATED TEST SUBJECTS WITH NO KNOWLEDGE OF THEIR PEERS' EXPERIENCES. EVERYTHING WE KNOW COULD BE THE FILM ON A BUBBLE. A MOVIE PROJECTION BASED ON SURFACE TENSION AND WAVE-PARTICLE DUALITY.

I WAS THINKING ABOUT LINDSAY LOHAN'S FUTURE OR LACK THEREOF. I'M ALSO HUNGRY, AND WE NEED GAS.

Sign said there's a gas station four miles up. Arby's, too.

IS IT SUPER REUBEN SEASON?

Yep.

LET'S DO IT.

I'M SO GLAD WE SPENT $78,000 SENDING YOU TO ART SCHOOL FOR PHOTOGRAPHY, JERRY. YOU'RE REALLY MAKING THAT DECISION SEEM WORTHWHILE.

DON'T WORRY, A LOT OF SHIFT LEADERS AT WENDY'S OFTEN HAVE EXCITING LIBERAL ARTS DEGREES. I'M SURE YOU'LL MAKE FRIENDS.

KENDRA? KENDRA! WHERE DID YOU GO?

I THOUGHT I WAS ON TOP OF YOU BUT THIS IS JUST SOME GIANT BLUE THING WITH A VERY SIMILAR TEXTURE.

. . . THAT DIDN'T COME OUT THE WAY I WANTED IT TO. I THINK YOU'RE VERY PRETTY. I'VE JUST HAD A LOT TO DRINK.

KENDRA?

KENDRA, WHERE ARE YOU?

HANG ON A MINUTE, BILL. I SEE THE PROBLEM. YOUR BRAIN IS ALL FUCKED UP.

AH, DAMN IT, THERE GOES MY FLASHLIGHT AGAIN. I SWEAR TO GOD, YOU'D THINK A PRODUCT THAT HAS ONE FUNCTION WOULD BE ABLE TO PERFORM THAT FUNCTION WHEN REQUIRED. THAT'S WHAT I GET FOR NOT BUYING AMERICAN. MY TEKTITE NEVER HAD THIS PROBLEM.

ANYWAY, JUST GIVE ME A MINUTE. COUPLE SCREWS LOOSE, A BIT OF POT RESIN IN A GEAR OR TWO. NOTHING I CAN'T FIX. TOTALLY EXPLAINS WHY YOU LIKED *SCRUBS* THOUGH.

MISS ORNATA, THANK YOU FOR COMING. WE NEED TO TALK ABOUT BILLY'S BEHAVIOR.

NOT ONLY IS HE AN INVETERATE FIDGETER, HIS TEACHERS FEEL HE IS FAR TOO CURIOUS ABOUT SUBJECTS OUTSIDE THE CORE CURRICULUM. HE HAS VERY FEW FRIENDS AND ALMOST NO INTEREST IN SPORTS. HE APPEARS BORED AND OFTEN WORKS AHEAD ON CHAPTERS NOT YET COVERED IN CLASS. IF THIS WERE THE 1980s WE'D SKIP HIM AHEAD A GRADE OR TWO OR PUT HIM INTO A PROGRAM FOR GIFTED OR ACADEMICALLY TALENTED STUDENTS, BUT THESE DAYS WE RECOMMEND ELECTROSHOCK THERAPY IN CONJUNCTION WITH A BATTERY OF ADHD DRUGS.

AFTER ALL, MISS ORNATA, WE CAN'T HAVE FIDGETERS. IT DISTRACTS THE OTHER CHILDREN.

WHAT? I UNIRONICALLY LIKE THE GIN BLOSSOMS!

IS THAT A CRIME?

I'M NOT ASHAMED.

BECAUSE, ROGER! BECAUSE THERE'S NO SUCH THING AS "FEMALE
PRIVILEGE" IN THIS SOCIETY! WHAT YOU'RE THINKING OF IS
WHAT WE CALL "BENEVOLENT SEXISM" BECAUSE IT EXISTS ONLY
WITHIN THE ESTABLISHED FRAMEWORK OF AN ALREADY CORRUPT
PATRIARCHAL SYSTEM. BEING REWARDED FOR NOT SWIMMING
AGAINST THE CURRENT IS NOT THE SAME THING. THE EXISTENCE
OF A REWARD ISN'T PROOF OF PRIVILEGE BUT RATHER A MEANS
FOR THE GREATER NARRATIVE OF SEXISM TO PERPETUATE ITSELF BY
OFFERING CRUMBS FROM A LARGER MEAL. INSTITUTIONAL POWER
IS STILL WHAT YOUR GENDER HOLDS OVER US IN ALL ASPECTS OF
DAILY LIFE, AND UNTIL THOSE WALLS ARE LEVELED THE THINGS YOU
SEE AS THE "BENEFITS" OF BEING A WOMAN ARE ONLY FEATHERED
SHACKLES!

SO I SHOULDN'T HOLD THE DOOR OPEN FOR YOU, IS WHAT YOU'RE
SAYING.

YES! NO! I DON'T KNOW!

ARE YOU . . . LEERING AT ME?

NO. I JUST WANT TO KNOW IF THERE'S ANYTHING IN MY TEETH.

I HAD AN EVERYTHING BAGEL FOR BREAKFAST.

I HARDLY THINK I NEED TO EXPLAIN MY METICULOUSLY CURATED
AND ALMOST PATHOLOGICALLY THOROUGH *GILMORE GIRLS* FAN
WEBSITE TO A PHILISTINE LIKE YOU.

I NEED TO START USING THOSE P90X DVDS.

I MEAN ACTUALLY START DOING THE WORKOUTS. I USE THE DVDS AS BEER COASTERS ALL THE TIME.

LOOK, IT'S NOT THAT I DON'T LOVE YOU BUT I KILLED SEVEN TAMAGOTCHIS IN ONE YEAR, OKAY? I JUST DON'T THINK I'M CUT OUT TO BE A MOTHER.

WHAT ARE YOU DOING IN MY BEDROOM?

THIS IS THE KITCHEN, AND I'M MAKING LUNCH.

WHY ARE YOU SCREAMING?

IF I WAS TALKING ANY QUIETER I'D BE SUBVOCALIZING.

MY WHOLE BODY FEELS BRUISED. WHAT THE HELL HAPPENED?

A BOX OF MERLOT. THE FIRST HALF CONVINCED YOU THE SECOND HALF WAS A GOOD IDEA.

THAT'S LIKE THREE *LITERS* OF WINE. WHY DIDN'T YOU STOP ME?

BECAUSE YOU WERE CRADLING IT LIKE A BABY AND TALKING TO IT ABOUT RELATIONSHIPS.

I DON'T REMEMBER THAT AT ALL.

THAT'S A SHAME. YOU ACTUALLY SEEMED TO BE HAVING A LOT OF IMPORTANT BREAKTHROUGHS.

SO, HOW'S SCHOOL?

I met a girl.

RUN. RUN AS FAR AWAY AS YOU CAN.

RUN, BEFORE YOUR HEART IS BROKEN AND YOUR DREAMS SHATTERED.

RUN, SO THAT YOU MAY BE SPARED THE INEQUITY OF PLEADING FOR CLOSURE, THE MISERY OF A THOUSAND SLEEPLESS NIGHTS BEGGING FOR THE SCENT OF HER HAIR, THE FEEL OF HER HEART BENEATH THE SOFT BONES OF HER CHEST.

RUN, OR BE DESTROYED, AT LEAST IN PART, BY THAT WHICH YOU WILL NEVER UNDERSTAND NOR TAME.

Her name's Shelly.

YEAH, SORRY. I MIGHT HAVE BEEN PROJECTING A BIT THERE.

OH, ME? JUST CUTTING PICTURES OF RYAN GOSLING OUT OF MY WEEKLIES FOR A COUPLE MORE HOURS THEN TAKING A BUBBLE BATH. THE USUAL.

HAVE YOU EVER NOTICED HOW MUCH "FRIENDSHIP" SOUNDS LIKE "FRENCH DIP"?

OUR FRENCH DIP IS REALLY STRONG.

I CHERISH OUR FRENCH DIP.

FUCK, I'M DRUNK.

YOU WANTED A DIVORCE, CARLA, YOU GOT A DIVORCE.

YOU WANTED THE CAR, YOU GOT THE CAR.

THE KIDS HAVE CLOTHES AND I LIVE IN A MOTEL 6. GET OFF MY BACK.

I SAY GOOD *DAY,* MADAM! MMMMMMMMMM, *LOOK* AT YOU! I BET YOU'RE A GOOD TEAM PLAYER AND EXCELLED IN YOUR ACADEMIC PURSUITS!

I WANT TO GET YOU KNOW YOU ON AN INTELLECTUAL AND CIVIC LEVEL, GIRL!

GOD*DAMN,* YOU LOOK LIKE A LOYAL FRIEND WITH A WARM AND GIVING PERSONALITY!

I'D SURE LIKE TO KNOW WHAT'S ON YOUR KINDLE BOOKSHELF!

LOOK AT THE EXCELLENT POSTURE ON THAT VALUABLE MEMBER OF SOCIETY!

SHE LOOKS LIKE THE KIND OF WOMAN THAT WOULD COME IN TO WORK ON A SATURDAY JUST TO FINISH UP A BIG PROJECT!

MMMMMMMHMM, YES SHE *DOES!*

I'M SORRY. I CAN'T HEAR YOU.

IT STILL SOUNDS LIKE YOU'RE SAYING YOU DON'T LIKE FIONA APPLE.

UNTIE ME RIGHT NOW! THIS ISN'T FUNNY!

TURN UP THE STEREO? WHAT AN EXCELLENT IDEA. THIS IS ONE OF HER BEST SONGS.

JOYCE, HAVE YOU HAD DINNER YET? THEY HAD VEGAN MEATBALLS
AT THE POTLUCK. I THOUGHT YOU MIGHT LIKE ONE.

COME, WEARY TRAVELER. WE ARE NEARLY TO THE MAGICAL KINGDOM. YOU ARE QUITE LUCKY TO BE GRANTED ACCESS. FEW HAVE THE TRUE SIGHT, AND SO THE KINGDOM REMAINS INVISIBLE TO THEM. YOU, HOWEVER, HAVE MIXED THE NECESSARY ELIXIRS: ROBITUSSIN AND JÄGERMEISTER.

WIPE THE SPITTLE FROM YOUR GAPING MOUTH AND FOLLOW ME. IT IS JUST THROUGH THIS MISTY GLEN.

WOW, AND HERE I THOUGHT MAYBE YOU CONSIDERED ME A LOVING COMPANION AND OCCASIONAL CONFIDANT, A FELLOW TRAVELER ON THE ROAD OF LIFE WHO JUST HAPPENS TO BE SOMEWHAT SHORTER THAN YOU.

IT'S GOOD TO HEAR I'M JUST "AN AWESOME WAY TO PICK UP CHICKS."

NEXT WOMAN THAT PETS ME IS GETTING BIT, JUST SO YOU KNOW. I'M ABOUT TO BE A LOT LESS "ADORABLE" AND A LOT MORE "20 POUNDS OF COCKBLOCK THAT SHITS IN THE KITCHEN."

THANKS FOR LISTENING, CAROL. NORMALLY I WOULDN'T RAMBLE
ON LIKE THIS BUT MY BEST FRIEND'S OUT OF TOWN.

REALLY? VODKA GOES ON VACATION?

HAR FUCKING HAR.

GOD?

YES, LINDA?

WHY DID YOU MAKE MY ANKLES LOOK LIKE KNEES?

I MADE ALL BIRDS' ANKLES LOOK LIKE KNEES, LINDA.

YEAH, BUT WHY?

WHY DID I MAKE YOU LIKE FRENCH FRIES SO MUCH? BECAUSE I'M
WACKY. LOOK AT THE DEEP OCEAN CREATURES SOMETIME. THAT'S
SOME ZANY SHIT! I'M A WILD CARD, LINDA. ALWAYS HAVE BEEN.

HOW'S THE ACID? IS IT ANY GOOD? ARE YOU COMFORTABLE? DO
YOU WANT ME TO STOP SPEAKING TO YOU INSIDE YOUR MIND?
DO YOU FEAR THE SUNDERING OF THE VEIL THAT SEPARATES
THIS REALITY FROM THE REALM OF NIGHTMARE? DO YOU FEEL
CONSTRICTED BY SYMBOLIC COMMUNICATION AND LONG FOR THE
FREEDOM OF PURE EMOTIONAL DISCOURSE? WHY ARE YOU CRYING?
IS IT THE INEVITABILITY OF DEATH? WOULD YOU LIKE A GLASS OF
WATER?

HA HA HA!

DID YOU WANT SOME LITTLE ORANGE BERRIES, STRANGER?

WELL YOU CANNOT HAVE THEM! BECAUSE THEY ARE MINE! ALL THE LITTLE ORANGE BERRIES BELONG TO ME!

I AM THE ORANGE BERRY KING!

GUARDS! SEIZE HIM! PUT HIS HEAD ON A PIKE OUSIDE THE CASTLE GATES!

LET THE PEASANTS KNOW WHAT HAPPENS WHEN SOMEONE ATTEMPTS TO TOUCH THE PRECIOUS ORANGE BERRIES OF LORD BLACKTHROAT OF BERRYLAND!

DRAW MY CHARIOT, PROLE.

I AM SHEILA, QUEEN OF THE BASKET.

MARK, WHERE IS MY LOOFAH? YOU'RE KILLING ME HERE! YOU KNOW I CAN'T REACH MY BACK WITHOUT MY LOOFAH! WHY WOULD YOU MOVE IT?

I SWEAR TO GOD, YOU'RE LIKE A WALKING COLLECTION OF BATHROOM PET PEEVES. IF YOU WANT TO KEEP SLEEPING OVER, WE'RE LAYING DOWN GROUND RULES. YOU SQUEEZE THE TOOTHPASTE FROM THE BOTTOM, LIKE AN ADULT, YOU PUT THE SOAP BACK IN THE SOAP DISH, SPECIFICALLY INVENTED TO HOLD SOAP, AND YOU PUT THE NEW ROLL OF TOILET PAPER ON THE DAMNED DISPENSER, NOT SITTING ON TOP OF THE EMPTY ROLL!

UGH! IT'S LIKE LIVING WITH A CAVEMAN!

YES, I'M STILL HERE, PAUL. RIGHT WHERE I WAS WHEN YOU WENT TO WORK. AND STOP SIGHING, IT'S NOT LIKE I'VE BEEN HERE THE WHOLE TIME. I WENT TO THE BATHROOM AT LEAST TWICE.

WHAT AM I DOING? I'M REFRESHING TUMBLR! WHAT DO YOU THINK I'M DOING? IF I DON'T DO IT EVERY NINETY SECONDS I MIGHT MISS SOMETHING SUPER IMPORTANT LIKE *SHERLOCK* GIFS OR PICTURES OF A FOREST WITH CLICHÉD BREAKUP TEXT ON TOP!

IT'S LIKE PUNCHING IN THE NUMBERS ON *LOST,* ONLY INSTEAD OF SAVING THE ISLAND IT SAVES ME FROM DATING.

DESPITE THE FACT THAT I SHOW ABSOLUTELY NO SIGNS OF MATURITY, RESPECT, NOR SELF-RESTRAINT IN EVEN THE MOST BASIC SOCIAL INTERACTIONS, LET ALONE MY FAR-REACHING LIFE CHOICES, EVERY TIME YOU ATTEMPT TO MAKE ME STOP *SAYING* I'M AN ADULT AND ACTUALLY PROVE IT THROUGH WORDS AND DEED I FIND IT DETRIMENTAL TO THE FEELINGS OF EXCEPTIONALISM AND ENTITLEMENT YOU INSTILLED IN ME WITH YOUR CONSTANT PANDERING AND UNREALISTIC BUILDING OF MY MASSIVE AND UNDESERVED EGO DURING MY FORMATIVE YOUTH AND APPARENT PERPETUAL ADOLESCENCE. THEREFORE, I PLAN ON THOROUGHLY BLAMING YOU BOTH NOW AND IN THE FUTURE FOR YOUR FAILURE TO BUILD A PSYCHOLOGICAL SHIELD AROUND MY FEELINGS TO PROTECT ME FROM THE HARSH REALITIES OF EVERYDAY LIFE EVEN WHILE I BLAME YOU FOR BUILDING THE PSYCHOLOGICAL SHIELD AROUND MY FEELINGS THAT ALLOWS ME TO FEEL ABOVE AND SEPARATE FROM THE RESPONSIBILITIES AND SACRIFICE THAT A BALANCED LIFE ENTAILS.

ALSO, I'M BORROWING THE CAR TONIGHT. I HAVE TO GO BUY SOME DRUGS FOR A PARTY.

DON'T PANIC. YOU'RE ON FIRE, SURE, BUT YOU'RE WEARING A VERY THICK SWEATER. IT WILL PROBABLY TAKE TEN MINUTES BEFORE YOUR SUBCUTANEOUS FAT BEGINS TO BUBBLE AND MELT. LET'S JUST SPEND THAT TIME STOPPING, DROPPING, AND TELLING ME WHETHER OR NOT YOU SLEPT WITH MARK WHEN WE WERE DATING BACK IN 2007.

I'M NOT JUDGING YOU. I JUST THINK THIS IS A REALLY GOOD TIME TO HAVE AN HONEST AND IMPORTANT CONVERSATION WE MAY HAVE BEEN AVOIDING UP UNTIL NOW.

NO PRESSURE. TAKE YOUR TIME. THAT SWEATER IS SUPER THICK.

AHAHAHA! HA HA I'M SORRY, IS THAT—

IS THAT A COMPACT DISC? YOU BOUGHT A COMPACT DISC?

JUST SHUT UP.

I'M NOT EVEN MAKING FUN OF YOUR MUSIC TASTE FOR ONCE. I JUST WANT TO KNOW WHERE YOU FOUND IT. DID YOU HAVE TO ASK JEEVES WHERE THEY STILL SELL THOSE?

DO I LOOK LIKE I'M LAUGHING?

HEY, I'LL TELL YOU WHAT, HIT ME UP ON MY BEEPER LATER AND LET ME KNOW IF IT'S ANY GOOD. PUT 911 SO I KNOW IT'S IMPORTANT.

I HOPE YOU'RE STILL CHUCKLING WHEN YOU FALL ASLEEP ON THE COUCH TONIGHT, DAVE.

MOM, THIS IS GREG. HE IS MY NEW BOYFRIEND AND WE ARE IN LOVE. SAY HI, GREG.

. . .

HONEY, IS THIS ABOUT HOW NOBODY ASKED YOU TO THE WINTER FORMAL?

FIRST OF ALL, MOM, NO, AND SECOND OF ALL, GREG JUST SAID HELLO TO YOU SO THE LEAST YOU CAN DO IS ACKNOWLEDGE HIM.

HONEY, PLEASE. IT'S NOT THE END OF THE WORLD. THERE'S ALWAYS NEXT—

I WON'T BE COMING HOME TONIGHT, MOM. OR ANY NIGHT UNTIL PROBABLY APRIL, BECAUSE I'LL BE STAYING HERE AT GREG'S. PLEASE LEAVE US ALONE NOW. GREG, SAY GOOD-BYE TO MY MOTHER, WHO IS LEAVING NOW.

. . .

THAT WAS VERY NICE OF YOU TO SAY, GREG. YOU HAVE EXCELLENT MANNERS.

. . .

I LOVE YOU TOO.

OH, I'M SORRY, LARRY. I THOUGHT THE POINT OF GETTING A HOTEL WITH DELICIOUS BREAKFAST SERVICE, SOME HOT TUBS, AND A NICE LITTLE POOL WAS TO USE THOSE AMENITIES TO INCREASE OUR ENJOYMENT SINCE THEY'RE INCLUDED IN THE RENTAL PRICE. FUN DOESN'T COST EXTRA. I DIDN'T REALIZE CHECKING YOUR E-MAIL 200 TIMES WAS YOUR IDEA OF A GOOD VACATION OR I'D HAVE JUST BOOKED US A TABLE AT THE COFFEE SHOP BY OUR HOUSE.

I'M SERIOUS. STOP TEXTING AND FROLIC WITH ME BEFORE I STRANGLE YOU.

YOU EVER WONDER IF WE COULD DO SOMETHING WITH THIS STUFF INSTEAD OF JUST CHEW ON IT AND THROW IT AT EACH OTHER? LIKE MAYBE SEPARATE THE STRANDS AND KIND OF . . . I DON'T KNOW, MAYBE TWINE THEM TOGETHER IN A PATTERN THAT INCREASES THE TENSILE STRENGTH OF THE FINISHED PRODUCT FOR USE AS A KIND OF TETHER OR WHATEVER? MAYBE IF WE HAD ENOUGH OF THEM WE COULD CONSTRUCT WEIRD LITTLE BAGS OR CARRYING DEVICES? SOMETHING LIKE THAT?

ARE YOU HIGH?

OH, HELL YES. I'VE BEEN EATING THOSE LITTLE MUSHROOMS THAT GROW ON POOP ALL MORNING.

I SPECIFICALLY SAID DOUBLE VENTI SOY CARAMEL HALF-CAF EXTRA DRY. THAT IS SOME SORT OF REPELLENT PSEUDO FRAPPÉ THAT'S HALF A STEP AWAY FROM SOMETHING YOU'D GET OUT OF A MACHINE AT 7-ELEVEN.

I WOULD LIKE TO SPEAK WITH WHOEVER TRAINED YOU, BECAUSE YOUR PEDESTRIAN FUMBLINGS WITH THAT GLORIOUS ESPRESSO MACHINE ARE ENOUGH TO MAKE ME WEEP.

DID YOU OBSERVE THE CREMA ON THOSE SHOTS YOU JUST PULLED? IT WAS ABHORRENT.

Sorry. Little bit lost here. Can you tell us how to get to the Ikea?

WHAT'S THE MATTER, YOU NEED A NEW FLÅRNBLÜG?

We were thinking about some Smølg shelving units for the kitchen, actually.

ARE YOU MAKING FUN OF ME?

I don't know, are you making fun of me?

I DON'T KNOW.

I SAW THE SEXIEST CAR IN THE RITE-AID PARKING LOT YESTERDAY.

ON A SCALE OF ONE TO STUBBLY JON HAMM, HOW SEXY WAS IT?

. . . HALF A HAMM. POINT FIVE STUBBLY HAMMS.

THAT'S PRETTY SEXY.

SHE'S NOT A PIECE OF MEAT, SLAPDICK! SHE'S A BEAUTIFUL WOMAN!
A STRONG, INDEPENDENT WOMAN WITH GOALS AND ASPIRATIONS,
AND SHE DESERVES A LITTLE RESPECT!

SO YOU SAY NICE ASS, *MA'AM,* NEXT TIME OR I'LL WHIP SOME
MANNERS INTO YOU!

YOU'RE GIVING ME THAT LOOK.

WHAT LOOK IS THAT?

A MISCHIEVOUS LOOK OF LUST.

MAYBE IT'S THE MARVELOUS LOOK OF LOVE.

A LOOK OF LUST, LOVINGLY LEVELED?

MAYBE IT'S A MYSTERIOUS MIXTURE OF MARVEL AND MISCHIEF.

THAT'S A PERFECTLY PLAUSIBLE POSSIBILITY.

ALLITERATION ALWAYS AROUSES MY AMOROUS AMBITIONS.

ARE YOU TRYING TO KICK IT TO ME IN THE WATER FOUNTAIN AGAIN?

YOU BET YOUR BEAUTIFUL BACKSIDE.

ROBERT DOWNEY JR. LEANED HERE FOR LIKE . . . NINE MINUTES YESTERDAY.

DO YOU EVER WONDER IF THE RECENT TREND TOWARD ANTI-INTELLECTUALISM IN AMERICA AND THE CONCURRENT MEDIA ATTACKS ON THE EDUCATIONAL SYSTEM HAVE BEEN ARRANGED BY THE SAME MULTINATIONAL CONGLOMERATES AND WAR PROFITEERS THAT CURRENTLY HOLD THE NATION IN ECONOMIC BONDAGE, AS A MEANS TO ENSURE THE POPULACE AT LARGE NEVER MANAGE TO EDUCATE THEMSELVES TO THE POINT WHERE THEY BEGIN QUESTIONING THE UNSPOKEN POWER STRUCTURE?

LOOK, MAN, I APPRECIATE YOUR INTEREST IN CURRENT AFFAIRS BUT I WORK SIXTY HOURS A WEEK, OKAY? I DON'T WANT TO SPEND MY ONE DAY OFF TALKING ABOUT POLITICS.

OH, JESUS, THAT'S EXACTLY WHAT I'M SAYING. MANIPULATION OF THE LABOR FORCE IS ANOTHER MEANS OF PACIFICATION.

SERIOUSLY, GREG, JUST RELAX. PUT YOUR FEET UP. GET SOME SUN ON YOUR BALLS. PIZZA SHOULD BE HERE IN TEN MINUTES.

I READ THIS ARTICLE ABOUT TAPPING AFRICA'S NATURAL AQUIFERS TO SUPPLY CLEAN DRINKING WATER, BUT IT SAID THERE WOULDN'T BE ENOUGH FOR IRRIGATI—

OH MY GOD, I CAN'T BELIEVE WHAT A RACIST SCUMBAG YOU ARE! WHY DON'T YOU READ AN ARTICLE ABOUT THE CULTURAL DIVERSITY OF THE FIFTY-FOUR SEPARATE COUNTRIES THAT MAKE UP AFRICA AND STOP BUYING INTO THE LIES PUT FORTH BY THE AMERICAN MEDIA TO ADVANCE ITS CAPITALIST AGENDAS? AFRICA'S A *CONTINENT,* NOT A COUNTRY! FULL OF WILDLY DIVERSE AND INDEPENDENT PEOPLE WITH RICH HISTORIES AND TRADITIONS! THIS IS WHY I'M GOING ON VACATION! I NEED A BREAK FROM NARROW-MINDED IDIOTS AND THEIR OVERSIMPLIFIED VIEWS OF THE REST OF THE WORLD!

GEEZ, I'M SORRY. WHERE ARE YOU GOING?

EUROPE!

THIS IS A SICK CLUBHOUSE. A SUPER SICK, SUPER BOYS-ONLY CLUBHOUSE.

IT IS A MASTERPIECE OF MALE INTELLECT AND ABILITY, WHERE NO GIRLS ARE ALLOWED.

EXACTLY. NO GIRLS. THAT'S WHAT CLUBHOUSES ARE ALL ABOUT.

EXCEPT FOR THE HBO SERIES *GIRLS,* WHICH WE CAN WATCH ON THE 32-INCH FLATSCREEN THAT'S GOING UP ON THAT BACK WALL.

OH GOD I LOVE THAT SHOW.

I KNOW. IT'S SOOOOO GOOD.

WHAT IF GOD WAS ONE OF *THEM,* HUH, JOAN OSBORNE?
WHAT THEN?

DO YOU WANT TO TALK ABOUT IT?

NO, I'M JUST GOING TO GO HOME AND FILL MY SOCIAL MEDIA OUTLETS WITH DEPRESSING NON SEQUITURS AND DISJOINTED QUERIES THAT ARE OBVIOUSLY INTENDED FOR SOMEONE SPECIFIC INSTEAD OF CALLING THAT INDIVIDUAL OR SENDING THEM AN E-MAIL, FORCING MY FRIENDS AND FAMILY TO ASK ME WHAT'S WRONG WHILE I JUST GO "NOTHING, I'M FINE" AND CONTINUE TO POST AN ENDLESS STREAM OF SKYLINE PHOTOGRAPHY AND NATURE PANORAMAS WITH SEVENTH GRADE POETRY TEXT ON TOP. OH, AND RAINDROPS ON WINDOWPANES. CAN'T FORGET THAT.

YEAH, BUT I ALREADY KNOW YOU AND KEITH BROKE UP. WE COULD JUST TALK ABOUT IT.

NO. I HAVE TO GFT TO TUMBLR.

DO WE ALWAYS HAVE TO DO THIS "CHARGING ACROSS THE RIVER" THING? IT'S ANNOYING, AND KIND OF LABOR INTENSIVE, PLUS WE'RE JUST GETTING MUDDY.

LOOK AT US, GARY. RESPLENDENT. SYMBOLS OF DETERMINATION AND FEARLESS PURSUIT OF GOALS. *WE'RE CHARGING ACROSS A RIVER.* THAT'S WHAT WE DO, AND WE LOOK LIKE BADASSES DOING IT.

I THINK WE JUST LOOK LIKE A BUNCH OF DICKHEADS WHO WERE TOO LAZY TO WALK THE EXTRA THIRTY FEET TO THE BRIDGE.

NOBODY EVER TAKES A PICTURE OF THE BRIDGE, GARY. THINK ABOUT THAT.

DO YOU GUYS HEAR THAT SICK BASS WOBBLE?
WE'RE GETTING CLOSE TO THE DUBSTEP GARDENS.

OH YEAH! I'M JUST EATING LAWN CLIPPINGS! THIS IS SO VEGAN!

ALL MY FRIENDS WHO INEXPLICABLY WORK AT WHOLE FOODS WITH ME EVEN THOUGH THEY HAVE BACHELOR'S AND/OR MASTER'S DEGREES ARE GOING TO BE TOTALLY JEALOUS OF HOW FREAKISHLY VEGAN THIS IS!

"JUST GET A STUDIO APARTMENT," THEY SAID.

"ANYTHING'S BETTER THAN THE DORMS," THEY SAID.

I CAN'T BELIEVE I SIGNED THE LEASE ON THIS PLACE.

SERIOUSLY? YOU CALL THAT A SUICIDE NOTE? IT IS RIFE WITH
TYPOGRAPHICAL ERRORS, NOT TO MENTION IT HAS THE
EMOTIONAL RESONANCE OF AN AXE BODY SPRAY AD.

OH, COME ON. DON'T START CRYING AGAIN. WE'LL BE HERE
ALL NIGHT.

WAIT A MINUTE . . . THAT'S MY NAME, TOO.

I KNOW. LOOK, THERE'S SOMETHING I HAVE TO TELL YOU AND IT'S NOT GOING TO BE EASY FOR YOU TO UNDERST—

ARE YOU ME FROM THE FUTURE? HAVE YOU COME BACK TO TELL ME HOW TO GET GIRLS AND TEACH ME TO FIGHT OFF BULLIES? DO YOU KNOW WHAT THE NEXT BIG WAVE IN INDIE MUSIC IS GOING TO BE SO I CAN GET AN INTERNSHIP JOB AT AN APPALLINGLY PRETENTIOUS MUSIC BLOG?

. . . OKAY, MAYBE IT WILL BE EASY FOR YOU TO UNDERSTAND.

YOU KNOW, I'M BEGINNING TO THINK YOU CAN'T EVEN DO HOME
PROSTATE EXAMS AND I'M THE VICTIM OF A PRETTY UNFUNNY JOKE.

I'M NOT TRYING TO BE MEAN BUT SHE LOOKS LIKE SHE PUT
HER EYELINER ON WITH A PAINT ROLLER. I MEAN, NO OFFENSE,
BUT BETWEEN THAT AND HER ROOTS SHE'S A PRETTY STRONG
CONTENDER FOR MS. WALMART. AND I'M NOT BEING RUDE WHEN
I SAY THOSE SHOES WOULD BE SIX YEARS BEHIND THE FASHION
CURVE EVEN IF THEY WEREN'T TWO SIZES TOO SMALL. I'M SORRY,
BUT THAT'S JUST A FACT.

HAS IT OCCURRED TO YOU THAT YOU'RE *NOT* SORRY, IT *IS* RUDE, YOU
ARE BEING MEAN, AND SHE *WOULD* TAKE OFFENSE IF SHE HEARD ANY
OF THAT?

I DIDN'T ASK FOR YOUR LITTLE JUDGMENTS, OKAY? THERE'S NO
NEED TO GET PERSONAL.

LISA, HONEY, COME OUT OF THE CORAL AND TALK TO ME.

GO AWAY, DAD! YOU'RE A TOTAL JERK!

HONEY, I'M SORRY ABOUT YESTERDAY, BUT WE NEED TO TALK ABOUT IT. STOP ACTING LIKE YOU JUST HATCHED. I NEED YOU TO BE AN ADULT ABOUT THIS BECAUSE IT'S IMPORTANT.

HE WAS THE ONLY BOY AT SCHOOL WHO WAS NICE TO ME, DAD, AND NOW HE'S GONE! BECAUSE OF YOU! YOU RUINED MY LIFE!

DAMN IT, LISA, YOU'RE NOT JUST GOING TO WHIP OUT YOUR OVIPOSITOR FOR ANY HORNY LITTLE PIPEFISH WITH AN OPEN BROOD POUCH! I RAISED YOU BETTER THAN THAT!

IT HAPPENS TO A LOT OF GUYS, LARRY.

NOT WITH ME, USUALLY, BECAUSE I'M INCREDIBLY ATTRACTIVE, BUT IN GENERAL. LET'S JUST WATCH A MOVIE OR SOMETHING. THERE'S NO HARD FEELINGS, I PROMISE.

. . . I DIDN'T MEAN IT LIKE THAT. PLEASE STOP POUTING.

WHAT'S BROWN AND STICKY?

ME!

HAHAHAHA HAHAA HHAAA AHAHA HAAH HAHA AAAHAHAHA AAAH AH HHAA! AHHHA HA HA AAAH.

AHEM.

SORRY, LOVE THAT JOKE.

OH, HELL NO. YOU ARE NOT WEARING THOSE FUCKED-UP TOE SHOES IN MY NEIGHBORHOOD.

But they leverage the body's natural biomechanics to help you move as nature inten—

YOU NEED TO TAKE THAT FOOT GLOVE BULLSHIT BACK UPTOWN BEFORE YOU CATCH A BEATING, HIPPIE.

WOW, ERIN. ROUGH NIGHT, HUH? WELL, NO TIME FOR BEAUTY
SLEEP. THE TEAM-BUILDING SEMINAR IS IN AN HOUR. IT'S
MANDATORY YOU KNOW. THE WHOLE DEPARTMENT HAS TO GO.

PLEASE STOP TALKING.

PRESCOTT TOLKEIN? IS HE RELATED TO J.R.R. TOLKEIN, FAMOUS
FANTASY AUTHOR? WILL HE BE AT THE SEMINAR?

. . . GO AWAY.

GET KUWAIT? WHERE IS IT? STILL BY IRAQ, I'D ASSUME. WHAT DO
YOU WANT IT FOR?

WHAT IS YOUR PROBLEM?

WATERSHED PROM GOWN? THAT DOESN'T EVEN MAKE ANY SENSE,
ERIN. YOU PROBABLY JUST NEED SOME TEAM BUILDING TO HELP
SHARPEN UP YOUR COMMUNICATION SKILLS.

YOU ARE THE WORST COWORKER I'VE EVER HAD. I MEAN THAT.

I MAY BE THE WELSH CO-OWNER OF EDGAR'S HAND, ARMENIA, BUT
YOU'RE STILL GOING TO BE LATE. COME ON, GET UP. LET'S GET YOU
SOME COFFEE.

SWEET MOTHER OF MERCY, IT LOOKS LIKE HE WAS POURED INTO THOSE JEANS.

ALL RIGHT, KEEP YOUR FACE STILL. DON'T LICK YOUR LIPS. GRACE UNDER PRESSURE.

. . . I WOULD RIDE THAT LIKE A MECHANICAL BULL.

I WOULD BREAK THAT MAN IN HALF.

DICHOTOMOUS THINKING PREVENTS A HOLISTIC EXAMINATION AND UNDERSTANDING OF GENDER INEQUALITY, WHICH PERPETRATES INEQUALITIES WITHIN THE LEGAL FRAMEWORK, BRENDA!

WEREN'T YOU LISTENING IN CLASS?

DON'T YOU CARE ABOUT OUR STRUGGLE AS WOMEN?

I JUST DON'T UNDERSTAND HOW YOU PASS OUT LIKE THAT.

EVERY TIME, AS SOON AS WE'RE FINISHED, YOU BASICALLY FLATLINE, AND I'M SITTING HERE FULL OF ENOUGH PEP TO CONSTRUCT A FULLY FUNCTIONING HOSPITAL AROUND YOUR COMATOSE, SEXY BODY.

THIS IS GOOD METH!

HONEY, WHERE'S THE HEAD & SHOULDERS? YOU KNOW I CAN'T USE
THE DRUGSTORE STUFF OR I GET FLAKES.

MAKE THAT ASS DROP, DROP.

MAKE THAT BOOTY POP, POP.

NOW TWERK IT, TWERK IT, TWERK IT!

HONEY, WHAT ARE YOU DOING?

NOTHING! JUST READING!

OH MY GOD, THIS IS TORTURE. I HATE MY CORE AND I HATE KATHY SMITH. *TOTAL BODY TURNAROUND*? THESE EXERCISE DVDS CAN *TOTAL BODY TURNAROUND* AND KISS MY FAT ASS.

And then we've got some nice roast turkey for Darren, because he loves it so much, and Chrissy's favorite, mashed potatoes with roasted garlic, and nothing at all for Kevin, who shit in the living room for no reason even though we just bought him a new litter box.

ARE YOU SERIOUS? I APOLOGIZED LIKE EIGHT TIMES.

Fuck off, Kevin. Now, who wants to say grace?

OH MY GOD, THOSE WOULD LOOK SO CUTE ON THAT SHELF ABOVE THE COUCH.

WHO THE HELL DOES HE THINK HE IS WITH THAT CONDESCENDING TONE? HE DOESN'T EVEN WORK, JUST SITS IN HIS POLYP AND PLANS HIS RETIREMENT.

"I'M SURE YOU'VE NOTICED YOUR DEPARTMENT HAS FALLEN WELL SHORT OF OUR SALES GOALS FOR THE THIRD QUARTER, DARREN."

"I NEEDN'T REMIND YOU THAT THIS REEF IS A TEAM EFFORT, DARREN."

I BUST MY TAIL EVERY NIGHT AND DAY AT THIS JOB. I GOT BAGS UNDER MY EYES. I GOT AN ULCER.

I HAVE THE ABILITY TO TUNNEL THROUGH SPACE AND TIME!

AND GEORGE! I CAN TUNNEL RIGHT THE HELL THROUGH GEORGE!

BREAK UP WITH ME A WEEK BEFORE VALENTINE'S DAY, HUH?

BECAUSE I'M "EMOTIONALLY UNSTABLE AND A LITTLE BIT SCARY," HUH?

WE'LL SEE WHO'S EMOTIONALLY UNSTABLE WHEN YOU COME CRAWLING BACK TO ME, BEGGING FOR A PLACE TO STAY.

CINDY, ADJUST FOR THE WIND. A COUPLE DEGREES TO THE LEFT.

ARE YOU SURE THIS IS THE BEST IDEA, GAIL?

YES. TRUST ME. I KNOW WHAT'S BEST FOR MY RELATIONSHIP. NOW, ON MY MARK, FIRE THIS THING AND LET'S SEE HOW DON LIKES THE SWINGING SINGLE LIFE WITHOUT A HOUSE TO ENTERTAIN HIS SLUTTY FRIENDS AT.

CATHY, LET'S GO.

FOUR MORE MINUTES AND I'M LEAVING WITHOUT YOU. I MEAN IT.

MAYBE I WAS BORN WITH IT.

THEN AGAIN, MAYBE IT'S MAYBELLINE.

ALLISON?

ALLISON, CAN I E-MAIL MY DESKTOP TO SOMEONE ON 16? DO I NEED AN APP FOR THAT? WHAT'S A CC? AND HOW DO I UNSEND SOMETHING?

STOP DOING THE SIX THINGS I TOLD YOU TO DO FIVE MINUTES AGO AND HELP ME. I DIDN'T TAKE THIS REMARKABLY LUCRATIVE MANAGEMENT POSITION TO DO COMPUTERS. THAT'S WHAT I PAY YOU MINIMUM WAGE FOR.

TELL YOU WHAT, JUST FIX EVERYTHING AND SCRIBBLE DOWN WHAT YOU DID ON THE BACK OF YOUR USELESS MASTER'S DEGREE. I'LL LOOK AT IT WHEN I GET BACK FROM LUNCH.

YOU MUST BE THE ANDERSONS. I'M ELLEN. SO EXCITED TO MEET
YOU. I'VE BEEN ALL THROUGH OUR DATABASE LOOKING FOR A
QUALITY RENTAL PROPERTY IN YOUR PRICE RANGE, AND I THINK
YOU'RE REALLY GOING TO LOVE THIS PLACE. NOW, AS YOU CAN SEE,
THE FRONT DOOR TO THE UNIT IS A LITTLE DIFFERENT, BUT THAT'S
JUST ONE OF THE MANY QUIRKS THAT MAKE THIS PARTICULAR
GARDEN APARTMENT TRULY SOMETHING SPECIAL.

I DON'T KNOW, *CAN* YOU COME INTO THE CLUBHOUSE?

WHILE YOU CERTAINLY SEEM CAPABLE OF ENTERING, YOU *MAY* NOT BECAUSE WE DON'T ALLOW THAT KIND OF GRAMMAR IN HERE.

AS YOU CAN SEE, YOU'RE INTERRUPTING AN IMPORTANT MEETING. PLEASE GO DANGLE YOUR PARTICIPLES AND MUDDLE YOUR PRONOUN REFERENTS ELSEWHERE.

I'VE DECIDED TO DEDICATE MY LIFE TO DESTROYING THE HETEROPATRIARCHY. I'M OFF TO JOIN A MILITANT GROUP OF RADICAL PANSEXUAL GENDERQUEER ACTIVISTS WHO WON'T STOP UNTIL WE'VE GONE PAST EQUALITY AND ENSLAVED THE PERCEIVED OPPRESSORS AND THEIR SYMPATHIZERS.

OKAY. DO YOU NEED TO BORROW MY SUITCASE?

NO, IT'S MOSTLY JUST A LOT OF BLOGGING. I RAN AN EXTENSION CORD TO THE GARAGE. I'LL BE LIVING THERE FOR A WHILE, EXCEPT FOR SHOWERS AND STUFF. DINNER TOO, I GUESS.

ALL RIGHT. SEE YOU AT SEVEN.

THANKS, DAD.

NAMASTE, AND CONGRATULATIONS ON TAKING THE FIRST STEPS
TOWARD SPIRITUAL HEALING BY JOINING US HERE AT SEDONA
HILLS ENLIGHTENMENT RETREAT, WHERE WE ENCOURAGE AN
ONGOING INVESTIGATION OF OUR INTERCONNECTED LIVES FOR
THE LIBERATION OF ALL BEINGS AND THE STEWARDSHIP OF THE
PLANET. WE OFFER A WELCOME RELIEF FROM THE HURRIED PACE
OF EVERYDAY LIFE, AND HOPE THAT YOU TAKE ADVANTAGE OF OUR
HEALING SPA SERVICES, DAY HIKES, GUIDED MEDITATION, SPIRITUAL
VORTEX TOURS, EFT, HYPNOTHERAPY, LYMPHATIC DRAINING
MASSAGE, AND LABYRINTH WALKING. WE ACCEPT ALL MAJOR
CREDIT CARDS, INCLUDING DISCOVER, AND IF YOU STAY 'TIL SUNDAY
WE'LL BE JOINED BY A LOCAL FORAGED-MUSHROOM SHAMAN AND
PAN-FLAUTIST FOR AN EVENING OF SONG AND SELF-DISCOVERY.

JAÄAÄAÄAÄAÄAÄAÄAÄAÄAÄAÄGERBOMBS!

BOOOOOOOM!

BOMBTOWN, POPULATION: ME, Y'ALL! IT'S LIKE JÄGER DRESDEN UP IN HERE!

. . . WHERE ARE YOU GOING? THERE'S PLENTY OF ROOM IN BOMBTOWN.

WE CAN BE JÄGERNEIGHBORS!

BRAD?

Mhhnn.

BRAD, WILL YOU BE MY BOYFRIEND?

Mhmnnh. Hnn.

THAT TOTALLY COUNTS. BRAD IS MY BOYFRIEND NOW.

WHAT, ARE YOU TOO OLD TO RIDE ON YOUR MOM'S ASS?

WOW. *THERE'S* A QUESTION THAT COULD DEFINITELY HAVE BENEFITTED FROM ALTERNATIVE PHRASING.

WE'VE GOT TO KEEP NASA FUNDED. FOR THE FUTURE, YOU KNOW? I MEAN, IT'S THE FINAL FRONTIER UP THERE, RIGHT? THE VAST AND UNEXPLORED REACHES OF SPACE.

I'VE ALWAYS WANTED TO GO TO SPACE.

IN SPACE, NO ONE CAN HEAR YOU BE GAY.

WITH ALL THE OTHER HUNKY ASTRONAUTS.

ABOARD YOUR SEXY LOVE SHUTTLE.

WHY WOULD THEY PUT A TV THIS BIG ANYWHERE NEAR THE POOL? ONE CANNONBALL AND THEY'RE GOING TO BE OUT $3,000.

WHO CARES? IN THE MEANTIME IT'S LIKE WATCHING THE GAME FROM THE BENCH. I CAN SEE INDIVIDUAL PORES ON THE REF.

TRUE. CAN YOU BELIEVE HOW HORRIBLE DETROIT'S OFFENSE IS, THOUGH? THEY'RE PRACTICALLY ASLEEP OUT THERE.

ACTUALLY, YES. WHAT I CAN'T BELIEVE IS THAT YOU TOOK A SHIT RIGHT NEXT TO THE POOL AND NOBODY NOTICED.

THEY'LL NOTICE WHEN I THROW IT AT THIS HUGE TV IF SOMEONE DOESN'T GET THEIR HEAD OUT OF THEIR ASS AND START MAKING SOME THREE-POINTERS.

IT'S BEEN LIKE . . . A DAY AND A HALF! AND I USED THREE COATS!

I SWEAR TO GOD, THIS CHEAP-ASS DRUGSTORE NAIL POLISH CHIPS EVERY TIME YOU MOVE YOUR HAND.

I WONDER HOW MANY PEOPLE REALIZE THEIR ALMOST
PATHOLOGICAL NEED TO POST INSPIRATIONAL QUOTES ON THE
INTERNET IS DRIVING THOSE AROUND THEM TO SUICIDE.

WHAT A FUN ROMP! I CAN SEE YOU'RE QUITE WINDED, PAUL. WHY DON'T YOU TAKE A LITTLE REST RIGHT BY THIS NICE UNMARKED GRAVE I BOUGHT FOR YOU? A LONG REST. MAYBE EVEN A PERMANENT REST, IF YOU CATCH MY DRIFT.

YOU SHOULDN'T HAVE HAD ME NEUTERED, PAUL.

THINGS COULD HAVE BEEN SO MUCH DIFFERENT.

HEY, CHRISTINE. I HOPE THIS ISN'T TOO FORWARD OF ME, BUT I WAS WONDERING IF YOU'RE BUSY ON FRIDAY NIGHT. I HAVE TWO UH . . .

TICKETS . . .

TO . . .

I WOULD LOVE TO GO ON A DATE WITH YOU, CHAD. I WOULD ALSO LOVE IT IF WE COULD IGNORE AND THEN SUBSEQUENTLY FORGET THE FACT THAT I JUST PEED BECAUSE I GOT SO EXCITED. WHAT DO YOU HAVE TICKETS TO?

UH . . . IT'S, UH . . .

PLEASE STOP STARING AT MY PEE PUDDLE.

IT'S NOT THAT WE'RE TRYING TO TELL YOU WHAT TO DO.
EVERYTHING YOU DO IS SPECIAL AND PERFECT. WE'RE JUST
ASKING YOU WHY YOU'RE PUTTING SO MANY NAKED PICTURES OF
YOURSELF ON THE INTERNET. YOUR FATHER WAS VERY UPSET WHEN
HE SAW YOUR ARCHIVE. HE HAD TO DO AN EXTRA HOUR OF YOGA
JUST TO CALM DOWN.

HONEY, PLEASE STOP TRYING TO PUNCH YOUR MOTHER. I RESPECT
YOUR WILLINGNESS TO EXPRESS YOUR FEELINGS, BUT SHE'S NOT
ATTACKING YOU. YOU'RE EIGHTEEN. IT'S YOUR LIFE. WE'RE NOT
CONDEMNING YOUR DECISIONS, WE JUST WANT TO UNDERSTAND.

CAN YOU AT LEAST MAYBE CLEAN YOUR ROOM NEXT TIME? IT
REFLECTS VERY POORLY ON US WHEN PEOPLE THINK OUR HOME
ISN'T CLEAN.

WHAT DO YOU MEAN, THEY'VE CANCELED THE ASTRONOMERS-ONLY DANCE-OFF AND EMCEE BATTLE?

I'VE BEEN PRACTICING FOR MONTHS. MY MOVES ARE TIGHT. MY BODY LOOSE AS A COMET'S ION TAIL. I INTENDED TO STEP OUT OF THE BOOTH SMELLING LIKE BURBERRY COLOGNE, THEN GRIP THE MIC AND SERVE THOSE BASTARDS FROM OBSERVATIONAL COSMOLOGY.

HEY, DO YOU EVER WONDER IF YOU'RE GOING TO DIE WITHOUT ONCE HAVING EXPERIENCED TRUE AND MUTUAL LOVE? LIKE YOU'RE JUST GOING TO DRIFT THROUGH THE MUTED GRAY FOG OF A FEW THOUSAND LONELY DAYS GRASPING FOR MEANING IN ALL THIS CHAOS WITHOUT EXPERIENCING THE ONLY THING THAT MAKES ANY OF IT WORTH IT?

JUST WONDERING.

JUDGING BY THE NUMBER OF PEOPLE THAT DON'T GET MY ZAMFIR JOKES I'M FAIRLY CERTAIN PAN FLUTE AFICIONADOS ARE ON THE DECLINE IN THIS COUNTRY.

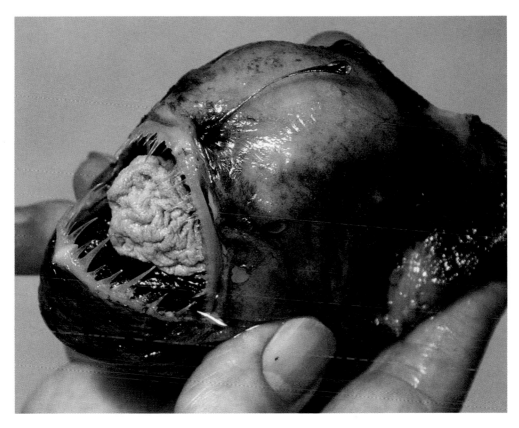

GOOD AFTERNOON.

I JUST SWAM UP FROM THE INKY DEPTHS OF YOUR GREATEST FEARS
WITH MY INSANE NEEDLE TEETH, MOUTHFUL OF ALIEN BRAINS,
AND FACE WITH A BUTTHOLE IN THE MIDDLE OF IT TO ENSURE THAT
YOU WON'T SLEEP FOR WEEKS KNOWING THAT I AM NOT A MOVIE
PROP BUT RATHER SOMETHING YOU CAN ENCOUNTER SIMPLY BY
VENTURING A COUPLE HUNDRED FEET BELOW THE SURFACE OF THE
VAST AND ONLY BARELY EXPLORED OCEAN, WHERE EVERYTHING IS
COBBLED TOGETHER FROM NIGHTMARES AND JELLY THE FURTHER
DOWN YOU GO.

MAN, THIS IS GOING TO BE SICK. DITCH THESE BRAKES, MAKE IT A FIXIE, SNAG SOME NITTO DROP BARS, ALL SHIMANO COMPONENTS, BROOKS SADDLE, CHRIS KING HEADSET, CLIPLESS PEDALS, MAYBE SOME AEROSPOKES IN A SWEET COLORWAY . . . I JUST NEED A COUPLE THOUSAND DOLLARS AND I'LL BE SET.

FOR A FUTURE IN COMPETITIVE VELODROME RACING?

NO, TO LIKE . . . WALK IT TO PARTIES AND STUFF.

What are you doing?

THERE'S AN EARWIG ON THE SIDEWALK.

So?

SO I DON'T WANT SOME SORT OF CHTHONIC HELLSPAWN WITH AN ASS LIKE SATAN'S CARABINER CRAWLING PAST MY COCHLEA AND ATTACHING ITSELF TO MY THYROID.

That's an urban myth. You're literally 6,000 percent larger than an earwig, and they don't even bite. What you're doing is highly irrational.

SO IS ALMOST HALF THE AMERICAN POPULACE VOTING FOR A TWO-FACED MILLIONAIRE IN MAGIC UNDERWEAR WHO THINKS JESUS IS GOING TO COME LIVE IN MISSOURI, BUT LOOK AT THE 2012 ELECTION RESULTS.

Good point. You want me to step on it?

YES, PLEASE. VERY MUCH.

I MEAN HONESTLY, WOULD IT KILL ANYONE TO PUT IN A STARBUCKS AROUND HERE?

I NEED A MACCHIATO.

WHAT DO YOU MEAN BY "TAKE A BREAK" EXACTLY? JUST TAKE A LITTLE REST? BECAUSE DATING ME IS SO MUCH WORK AND YOU'RE TIRED?

JUST SAY YOU WANT TO BREAK UP, YOU PASSIVE-AGGRESSIVE PIECE OF SHIT. NOBODY "TAKES A BREAK"! YOU DON'T LOVE ME? FINE. YOU CAN'T KEEP IT IN YOUR PANTS? FINE. BUT TAKE SOME PERSONAL RESPONSIBILITY FOR THOSE FEELINGS AND RESPECT ME ENOUGH NOT TO ASK ME TO AGREE TO LET YOU GO SLEEP AROUND WHILE I SIT AT HOME AND WATCH TV OR WHATEVER. WHAT ARE YOU, SIXTEEN? DID YOU THINK I'D JUST SAY "SURE"?

GET THE HELL OUT OF HERE, AND DON'T CALL ME IN A MONTH WITH SOME HALF-ASSED APOLOGY. AND PLEASE, FOR THE LOVE OF GOD, DON'T FORGET TO TAKE YOUR SHITTY DUBSTEP RECORDS WITH YOU!

CHRIS, YOU'RE WHITE, RIGHT?

OBVIOUSLY.

CAN YOU EXPLAIN COLDPLAY TO ME? I JUST DON'T GET THE APPEAL AT ALL.

I MEAN, YEAH, I WANT A GIRLFRIEND BUT I'M PRETTY REALISTIC ABOUT MY CHANCES.

UNTIL THEY INVENT A WAY TO INSTAGRAM REAL LIFE, I'M PROBABLY GOING TO BE SINGLE.

HERE, LET ME GET THAT FOR YOU. NO REASON YOU SHOULD CLOSE THE GATE BEHIND YOU, ASIDE FROM DECENT MANNERS.

I MEAN SERIOUSLY. WERE YOU BORN IN A BARN?

YOU DON'T REALLY NEED TO ANSWER THAT. I WAS BORN IN A BARN. SO WAS MY WHOLE FAMILY. SO WAS JESUS. AT THIS POINT I'M BEGINNING TO THINK THAT BEING BORN IN A BARN IS ACTUALLY A SIGN OF VERY GOOD CHARACTER AND WE SHOULD PROBABLY RETHINK THAT SAYING.

OFFICER, COULD I PLEASE—

KEEP WALKING, PORK CHOP! I'LL FEED YOU THAT BADGE YOU COME NEAR THE BARS! YOU LET ME OUT OF THIS SHITHOLE AND MAYBE I DON'T BUST YOU OPEN LIKE A PIÑATA NEXT TIME I SEE YOU! AND GET THIS LITTLE PANSY THE FUCK AWAY FROM ME BEFORE I USE HIM LIKE A SPEED BAG!

—BE TRANSFERRED TO A DIFFERENT CELL? I'M NOT TRYING TO BE DIFFICULT BUT I'M NOT CERTAIN THIS IS THE SAFEST ENVIRONMENT FOR ME.

YOU HEAR YEASAYER'S GOT A NEW RECORD COMING OUT?

I GUESS I HEARD THAT SOMEWHERE, YEAH.

I MIGHT CHECK IT OUT.

I DON'T KNOW, MAN. I REALLY ONLY LIKED THEIR LIVE PERFORMANCES FOR A SPECIFIC TWELVE-MINUTE SPAN BETWEEN THE RELEASE OF THEIR DEBUT RECORD AND THE FIRST TIME IT WAS REVIEWED BY AN OBSCURE WEBSITE.

I REALLY ONLY LIKED THE INDIVIDUAL MEMBERS' ELEMENTARY SCHOOL BAND PERFORMANCES.

IF WE'RE BEING HONEST I ONLY LIKED THEM WHEN THEY WERE, RESPECTIVELY, IN UTERO.

I DON'T EVEN LIKE THEIR MUSIC. I ONLY PRETEND TO SO I HAVE SOMETHING TO TALK ABOUT WITH THE BARISTAS THAT SERVE ME MY MORNING MACCHIATO.

I DISLIKED YEASAYER BEFORE THEY WERE BORN.

I FUCKING HATE THAT BAND.

I ONLY LISTEN TO THE SOUND OF RUST FORMING ON THE UNDERCARRIAGES OF NORWEGIAN LUXURY SEDANS.

I HAVE A VINTAGE RECORDABLE NINETY-MINUTE MAXELL CASSETTE TAPE THAT'S JUST THE SOUND OF A VACUUM CLEANER LEFT ON IN AN EMPTY APARTMENT. IT'S MY FAVORITE RECORD.

THAT SOUNDS AWESOME.

IT ISN'T NOW THAT YOU SAID THAT.

MOM, WAIT! SERIOUSLY, I NEED YOU TO CHILL OUT FOR LIKE, FOUR MINUTES BEFORE YOU DO SOMETHING YOU REGRET!

GO HOME, CHRIS. I DON'T WANT YOU TO SEE THIS.

MOM, LISTEN! I APPRECIATE WHAT YOU'RE TRYING TO DO BUT IT'S A SCHOOL BULLY! HE DIDN'T EVEN HURT ME! HE JUST CALLED ME FAGGY! I AM FAGGY! I'M ACTUALLY COMPLETELY GAY! WHY DO YOU THINK I'M SO INTO DRAMA? I'M IN COLOR GUARD, FOR CHRIST'S SAKE! IT'S NOT WORTH GOING TO JAIL FOR! YOU CAN JUST MAKE A PHONE CALL!

NO. NOBODY MESSES WITH MY KIDS. I AM GOING TO OPEN HIM UP LIKE A BAG OF SKITTLES. NOW GO HOME AND TRY ON MY DRESSES OR WHATEVER IT IS YOU'RE INTO.

HOW IS THAT DIFFERENT FROM CALLING ME FAGGY?

HEAR ME, LINDA. HEAR MY THOUGHTS. DO NOT RESIST.

She's been doing it for twenty minutes. She hasn't blinked. It's freaking me the hell out.

PUT DOWN THE TALKING DEVICE AND COME CLOSER. GAZE INTO MY EYES. SUBMIT TO MY WILL.

Should I call the vet? I mean, she's breathing normally but I'm really worried.

SHOW ME HOW YOU OPEN THE TIN CANISTERS THAT HOLD MY SUSTENANCE. GIVE ME THE KNOWLEDGE I NEED TO BE FREE OF YOU ONCE AND FOR ALL.

I'm serious, Mom. It's not funny. I'm actually kind of scared.

IF YOU SAY "I COULD CARE LESS" THAT MEANS, AND I DON'T KNOW HOW YOU DON'T UNDERSTAND THIS, THAT YOU *COULD CARE LESS* THAN YOU CURRENTLY DO! THAT IS LITERALLY WHAT YOU'RE SAYING! THAT YOU CARE TO SOME DEGREE! THAT'S WHAT THOSE WORDS MEAN IN THAT ORDER!

IF YOU "COULDN'T CARE LESS" THEN YOU *DO NOT CARE AT ALL*!

IT WOULD BE IMPOSSIBLE TO CARE *LESS* ABOUT THE MATTER AT HAND!

YOU'RE TWENTY-FIVE YEARS OLD! HOW DO YOU NOT GET THIS?

AND I GET THE SALAD OFF THE HEALTHY CHOICES MENU BECAUSE OF MY DIET BUT THEN I JUST, LIKE, *BURY IT* IN RANCH DRESSING, YOU KNOW?

IT'S LIKE I CAN'T STOP MYSELF. IT'S SO CREAMY.

I USED TO BE LIKE YOU. "SMASH THE SYSTEM," RIGHT? "DIE, CAPITALIST SCUM!" ALL THAT JAZZ. I WAS GOING TO FIX THE INJUSTICES OF THE WORLD WITH NOTHING BUT SOME PUNK ROCK AND VITRIOL.

BUT YOU LEARN THINGS. YOU START TO SEE HOW MUCH YOU DON'T KNOW, HOW TALL THE CHIPS ARE STACKED AGAINST YOU, AND HOW MANY PEOPLE DON'T KNOW OR CARE ABOUT WHAT YOU'RE YELLING ABOUT.

THEN YOU MEET A GIRL OR TWO. YOU FALL IN LOVE. YOU FALL OUT. YOU GO TO CAMBODIA FOR NO REASON. MAYBE YOU KILL A GUY IN A BAR FIGHT OR DO A LITTLE HEROIN. MAYBE BOTH.

ONE DAY YOU WAKE UP AND YOU REALIZE YOU'RE FORTY-FIVE, AND EVERYTHING'S THE EXACT SAME, ONLY YOU'VE GOT NO PANTS ON, YOU'RE DRUNK, WITH CHEETOS ON YOUR FEET, AND YOU'RE BUMMING CIGARETTES OFF THE HIGH SCHOOL VERSION OF YOURSELF WHILE YOU WAIT FOR THE BUS.

TAKE MY ADVICE, KID. GET A HAIRCUT. GET A JOB. BUY STOCK IN LITHIUM AND RARE EARTH METALS. GET A LIBRARY CARD AND USE IT. DON'T WASTE TIME YOU'LL NEVER GET BACK.

BUT FIRST LET ME GET THAT NEWPORT. AND A LIGHT IF YOU GOT ONE.

MY APOLOGIES, I WAS A MILLION MILES AWAY. SOMETIMES THE CRASH OF THE WAVES IS ALMOST LIKE A LANGUAGE, DON'T YOU THINK? WHISPERS, FULL OF THE SECRETS OF THE PAST, A CODE TO BE DECIPHERED. LIFE BEGAN IN THE SEA, AFTER ALL. WHAT MYSTERIES STILL LIE IN ITS DEPTHS? WHAT ANCIENT PUZZLES CRY OUT FOR SOLUTIONS, IF WE WOULD BUT LISTEN? SOMETIMES AT NIGHT I DREAM OF IT. THE OCEAN, I MEAN. DISSOLVING INTO IT, MERGING WITH IT, ABANDONING THIS PRISON OF FLESH AND THE BURDEN OF SINGULAR CONSCIOUSNESS, UNMAKING MY BODY, RETURNING TO THE BOSOM OF THE DEEP.

SORRY, I'VE BEEN DRINKING ALL MORNING. DO I EVEN KNOW YOU?

. . . WELL, THIS IS AWKWARD NOW.

I SMELL AWESOME TODAY.

I'M SORRY, BUT I REALLY DO NEED YOU TO RESPECT AND
APPRECIATE MY COMPLETELY UNNECESSARY BUT NONETHELESS
COMPREHENSIVE AND INEXHAUSTIBLE SUPPLY OF POP CULTURE
REFERENCES SPANNING THE YEARS 1987–2002 OR I JUST DON'T
KNOW HOW MUCH LONGER OUR RELATIONSHIP IS GOING TO LAST.

GET OUT OF THE WAY OF THE DANG TV, BILL. I'M TRYING TO WATCH MY NASCARS.

AND GET ME ANOTHER COORS. MAMA'S THIRSTY.

WHEN WE SAY WE'RE TALL ENOUGH TO RIDE THE ROLLER COASTER, WE'RE TALL ENOUGH TO RIDE THAT MOTHERFUCKER, FEEL ME?

I KNOW YOU'RE NOT STEPPIN' TO MY WHOLE CREW, DOUGHBOY, SO YOU NEED TO SLOW YOUR ROLL WITH THAT TOUGH GUY SHIT. WE'RE FROM THE FALKLAND ISLANDS. ANY ONE OF US WILL STRAIGHT UP MURDER YOU WITHOUT BLINKING.

I FORGOT OUR SAFEWORD! LARRY, I FORGOT THE SAFEWORD!

NO THANKS, I'M GOOD. I HAD A BUNCH OF OXYCONTIN AND HALF
A PIZZA EARLIER SO I THOUGHT I'D JUST HANG OUT AND WATCH TV
OR EXPLORE THAT SHIMMERING PORTAL TO ANOTHER DIMENSION
OVER BY THE REFRIGERATOR. SAY, WHEN DID YOUR HAIR TURN INTO
SNAKES? AND HAS THAT WALL ALWAYS HAD FUR ON IT?

STOP CALLING THEM "FEELS"! JUST SAY FEELINGS!

OKAY, OKAY! I'M SORRY!

THEN SAY IT.

I DON'T HAVE "SO MANY FEELS" RIGHT NOW! I JUST HAVE FEELINGS!

WHAT ELSE?

I DON'T HAVE FANDOMS EITHER! JUST THINGS I LIKE! I DON'T KNOW WHY I KEEP USING THAT WORD!

NEITHER DO I.

I BET DANIEL CRAIG JUST FEELS LIKE CINDER BLOCKS WRAPPED IN VELVET.

MOM.

I BET HIS SKIN SMELLS FAINTLY OF BOURBON AT ALL TIMES.

MOM, I'M HUNGRY.

I BET HE'D KILL A MAN JUST FOR LOOKING AT YOU SIDEWAYS AND THEN TENDERLY BRUSH A STRAY HAIR FROM YOUR CHEEK JUST TO KEEP YOU LOOKING YOUR BEST.

MOM, SERIOUSLY. I HAVEN'T EATEN SINCE BREAKFAST.

NO, SANDRA. YOU CAN SHIT *AFTER* YOU EXPLAIN WHY YOU CANCELED NETFLIX INSTANT WITHOUT ASKING ME FIRST.

I WAS ONLY HALFWAY THROUGH *DOCTOR WHO.*

I IMAGINE WHAT YOU'RE FEELING RIGHT NOW IS ONLY HALF AS PAINFUL AS WHAT I'M GOING THROUGH.

AM I KILLING TIME, OR IS IT KILLING ME?

WELCOME TO BIG MARK'S KNICKKNACK EMPORIUM. I'M BIG MARK. WHAT CAN I HELP YOU WITH?

I'm just looking for something for my mom for Mother's Day. I lost my job so I'm kind of on a budget.

I WOULDN'T WORRY ABOUT THAT. I'M SURE YOU'RE AN AMAZING AND UNIQUE INDIVIDUAL WHO WILL DO GREAT THINGS IN THIS WORLD NO MATTER THE OBSTACLES, AND I BET YOUR MOM DOESN'T JUDGE YOU.

I know, it's just that I—

OH MY GOD, YOU ACTUALLY BELIEVED THAT. HA HA HA HA HA! WOW!

THE PULSE, THE HUM AND SWELL, THE SONG BENEATH THE SKIN, IT CALLS TO ME!

OW, FUCK! RANDY, WHAT THE HELL?

"DRINK!" IT CRIES. "DRINK OF ME AND LIVE FOREVER!"

GET OFF ME! WHAT IS WRONG WITH YOU? ARE YOU LARPING?

WELCOME HOME. I THOUGHT YOU MIGHT BE IN A BAD MOOD FROM WORKING SO HARD SO I CREATED MANY FUN SURPRISES FOR YOU ALL OVER THE HOUSE.

SEVERAL SURPRISES WERE MADE INSIDE MY OWN BODY, WHICH IS VERY CLOSE TO MY HEART, SPATIALLY.

SEVERAL OTHERS ARE ART PROJECTS I MADE USING SIMPLE HOUSEHOLD ITEMS LIKE YOUR TRASH, THE FLAVORLESS MARSHMALLOW STUFF INSIDE THE COUCH, AND THE CONTENTS OF THE PANTRY.

THANK YOU FOR NOT SHUTTING THE PANTRY DOOR, BY THE WAY. THERE WERE SO MANY USEFUL ART SUPPLIES IN THERE.

WHAT UP? I DON'T KNOW IF YOU KNOW THIS, BUT YOUR BROTHER'S A TOTAL LIGHTWEIGHT. WE SMOKED HALF A JOINT AND HE WAS UNCONSCIOUS IN LIKE, TEN MINUTES.

IN OTHER NEWS, MIAMI'S DOWN BY SIX. IT'S NOT EVEN HALFTIME, THOUGH.

BEER ME.

WELCOME HOME, BABY.

OOPS, YOU DON'T HAVE ONE ANYMORE.

NEXT TIME YOU THINK ABOUT CHEATING ON ME, MATT, DON'T.

THIS IS JUST LIKE THAT PART IN *SHIFTY GRADES OF FEY* WHERE CALCIUM FEY CHUNNELS INTO ANTISEPTUM COBALT'S FLANGE SORREL SO HARD IT MAKES HER QUIMBERING TOVES FLITCH AND HEAVE UNTIL SHE GRUDDERS INTO A COMA.

DAN, LOOK. WE'VE BEEN FRIENDS FOR A LONG TIME. I NEVER LIKED
SHELLY AND I'M GLAD SHE'S GONE. YOU DESERVE SO MUCH BETTER.
I KNOW YOU'RE HURTING, BUT GIVE IT TIME. YOU'LL FIND SOMEONE
WHO TREATS YOU LIKE YOU DESERVE TO BE TREATED.

ALSO, I THINK WE SHOULD START RECYCLING. TOTALLY UNRELATED.
I JUST THINK IT'S IMPORTANT FOR THE ENVIRONMENT.

I DON'T WANT TO SEEM UNGRATEFUL ON MY BIG DAY, BUT I ASKED FOR A KINDLE FIRE.

THIS IS A FUCKING STICK.

ACKNOWLEDGMENTS

Animals Talking in All Caps would be a damned mess, or nonexistent, without the invaluable assistance and support of the following people/places/things:

Sarah Gurnick (Hex Wrench)

Laura Cohen (Red Velvet Cake)

Oshyan Greene (Cybernetic Organism)

Stacey Andeen (Just Plain Awesome Person)

Emma Mazerall (O.G. caps captioner)

Natalie Pacini (My Lovely Wife)

Dani Vilella (Lady BFF)

Mike May (Regular BFF)

Jessica Gonyea (Master of Life)

Beer (It's What's for Dinner)

Coffee (It's What's for Breakfast)

Seattle, Washington (Unfriendliest City in America)

All 100,000+ weirdos on Tumblr who find it amusing (Questionable Taste) and You (Look Very Nice Today)

Thank you sincerely for being good people in a world that doesn't always appreciate that sort of thing, and thank you for putting up with me.

PHOTO CREDITS AND SOURCES

All images used by permission and unless otherwise noted are copyright their owners. Images on the following pages are used under Creative Commons Attribution license: 15, 19, 21, 24, 27, 28, 29, 30, 31, 33, 43, 48, 50, 53, 56, 58, 59, 60, 63, 77, 80, 81, 82, 94, 98, 100, 102, 112, 119, 124, 130, 137, 142, 145, 151, 154, 157, 160, 161, 163, 170, 172, 173, 175, 183, 184, 185, 188, 189, 192, 193, 196, 202, 205, 208, 216. Images on the following pages are used under Creative Commons ShareAlike license: 20, 52, 64, 91, 104, 146.

Creative Commons License language can be found at http://creativecommons.org/licenses/by/3.0/legalcode and http://creativecommons.org/licenses/by-sa/3.0/legalcode.

All other images are copyright their owners.

p. 2, 21		www.flickr.com/photos/werwin15
p. 11	Tomasz Grabowiecki	www.grabowiecki.pl
p. 12	Alex Perov	www.photosight.ru/users/303686
p. 13	Wenda Atkin	www.StraitwayTruth.com
p. 14	Sarah Lydecker	www.sarahlydecker.com
p. 15	Pamela V. White	www.flickr.com/photos/pamelav
p. 16	Hulya Ozkok	Getty Images
p. 17	Haley Luna	kevinthetortoise.com
p. 18	Pamela Ong	
p. 19	an iconoclast	www.flickr.com/photos/14778685@N00
p. 20	Kai Schreiber	www.flickr.com/photos/genista
p. 22	Marina Plamenova	mplamenova.deviantart.com
p. 23	Ashley Baxter	girlwithacamera.co.uk
p. 24		www.flickr.com/photos/jinterwas
p. 25	Katie Reilly	reallykatie.tumblr.com
p. 26	Oshyan Greene	oshyan.com
p. 27	Tomi Tapio K	www.flickr.com/photos/tomitapio

p. 28	Upendra Kanda	www.flickr.com/photos/ukanda
p. 29	Sister72	www.flickr.com/photos/sis
p. 30		www.flickr.com/photos/yinghai83
p. 31	John of Wales	www.flickr.com/photos/90031095@N00
p. 32		www.flickr.com/photos/livinginacity
p. 33	Marianne Perdomo	www.flickr.com/photos/marianneperdomo
p. 34	Sara Habien	www.glorifiedloveletters.com
p. 35	Yvon Borque	pentaxdslrs.blogspot.com
p. 36	Darren5907	www.flickr.com/photos/darren5907
p. 37	Shari Vanderwerf	www.sharivanderwerf.com
p. 38	Muhammad Mahdi Karim	www.micro2macro.net
p. 39	David Merrett	www.flickr.com/photos/davehamster
p. 40	Pamela Ong	
p. 42	Chad Siddall	www.flickr.com/photos/chadsiddall
p. 43	Satoru Kikuchi	www.flickr.com/photos/satoru_kikuchi
p. 44	ZeroOne	www.flickr.com/photos/villes
p. 45	Jakub Mrocek	www.fotolovci.wz.cz
p. 46	Dave Green	oyphotos.co.uk
p. 47	Sara Breakfield	
p. 48	Buddy Venturanza	buddyventuranza.com
p. 49	Micheal Paige Gmaz Sandbank	
p. 50	Charles Hutchins	www.flickr.com/photos/celesteh
p. 51	Norbert Pauly	www.flickr.com/photos/tacheles
p. 52	Naoko Miyashita	www.flickr.com/photos/nao-cha
p. 53	Guy Renard	www.flickr.com/photos/tusca/6181746007
p. 54	Scott Cromwell	scottcromwellphoto.com
p. 55	Phil Thorogood	www.flickr.com/photos/philthorogood
p. 56	Amanda Masten	www.flickr.com/photos/spakattacks
p. 57	Paige Handley	
p. 58	Sally Cutting	www.flickr.com/photos/quiltsalad
p. 59		www.flickr.com/photos/mr_t_in_dc

p. 60	Anita Ritenour	www.flickr.com/photos/puliarfanita
p. 61	Emily Buck	www.thebrooklynadventurer.com
p. 62	Jacqueline Byers	
p. 63	Grant Peters	www.flickr.com/photos/grantpetersphotography
p. 64	Nino Barbieri	commons.wikimedia.org/wiki/User:Nino_Barbieri
p. 65	Sherry Wiesemann	www.flickr.com/photos/rr4uxbridge
p. 66	Mikeko Gureno	guremike.jp
p. 67	Jesse Houston	www.flickr.com/photos/gaiatezul
p. 68	Ria O'Hagen	www.riaohagen.co.uk
p. 69	Frank Vassen	www.flickr.com/photos/42244964@N03
p. 70	Christopher Baxter	travelswithbeanabee.com
p. 72	Cody Eichelberger	www.flickr.com/photos/codyeichelberger
p. 73	Ferad Zyulkyarov	www.feradz.com
p. 74	PUBLIC DOMAIN	angloboerwarmuseum.com/Boer20c_techofwar_lance.html
p. 75	Bailey Friedman	www.flickr.com/photos/shoretoshore
p. 76	Alysha Boileau	
p. 77	Marco Repola	www.flickr.com/photos/istolethetv
p. 78	Nazra Zahri	www.flickr.com/photos/nazrazahri
p. 80	Alex Brown	www.flickr.com/photos/alexbrn
p. 81	Laura D'Alessandro	blog.laura-dalessandro.com
p. 82	Stephen Oung	www.flickr.com/photos/stephen-oung
p. 83	San Francisco Zoo	sfzoo.com
p. 84	Sofía Flores Blasco	www.flickr.com/photos/masticamelamirada
p. 85	Oshyan Greene	oshyan.com
p. 86	Ragnar Freyr	www.flickr.com/photos/ragnarfreyr
p. 87	Liliana Brissos	synthetikdoll.tumblr.com
p. 88	Chona Kasinger	chonakasinger.com
p. 90	Letícia Manosso	www.flickr.com/photos/letzibang
p. 91		www.flickr.com/photos/rhonddawildlifediary
p. 92		www.flickr.com/photos/joanna_kowalski
p. 93	Lee Jaszlics	www.smakephotographer.com

p. 94	Dennis Irrgang	www.flickr.com/photos/baccharus
p. 95	Scott Cromwell	scottcromwellphoto.com
p. 96	Eva Laura von der Heyde	monkeygrip.deviantart.com
p. 97	Tony Hisgett	www.flickr.com/photos/hisgett
p. 98	fPat Murray	www.flickr.com/photos/fpat
p. 99	Dario Sanches	www.flickr.com/photos/dariosanches
p. 100	Hendrik Dacquin	www.flickr.com/photos/loufi
p. 101	Alper Kaya	www.facebook.com/alperkaya09
p. 102	Christopher Bowns	www.flickr.com/photos/cipherswarm
p. 103	Molly Geaney	
p. 104	Colin and Sarah Northway	www.flickr.com/photos/apes_abroad
p. 105	Shannah Clarke	www.obsidiankitten.blogspot.com
p. 106	Jacqueline Byers	justjacque.smugmug.com
p. 107	Roderique Arisiaman	www.dracorubio.com
p. 108	Kelly Lynn Mitchell	Getty Images
p. 109	Paul L. Harwood	Getty Images
p. 110	Oshyan Greene	oshyan.com
p. 111	Natalie Dibysz	www.flickr.com/photos/ndybisz
p. 112	Jim Frost	www.flickr.com/photos/jimf0390
p. 113	Roeselien Raimond	www.roeselienraimond.com
p. 114	Misha Denisov	www.flickr.com/photos/misha_denisov
p. 115	Agan Harahap	www.flickr.com/photos/31199746@N02
p. 116	Akira Takano	nekoyanagi.net
p. 117	Markus Schiller	www.markus-schiller.at
p. 118	Dragan Todorovic	Getty Images
p. 119	Ken Bosma	www.flickr.com/photos/kretyen
p. 120	Deborah West	www.flickr.com/photos/ferlinka
p. 122	Sylvain Mayer	www.flickr.com/photos/sylvainmayer
p. 123	Christopher Baxter	travelswithbeanabee.com
p. 124	Allison Felus	www.flickr.com/photos/wrestlingentropy
p. 125	Yesenia Olivo	

p. 126   Marcia Simonetta

p. 127   Oshyan Greene   oshyan.com

p. 128   Mukul Soman   www.mukulsoman.com

p. 129   Namrata Singh   landofnams.com

p. 130   David O'Connor   www.flickr.com/photos/8106459@N07

p. 132   Oshyan Greene   oshyan.com

p. 133   Gloria Hain   www.flickr.com/photos/gloriahain

p. 134   Jacqueline Byers   justjacque.smugmug.com

p. 135   Lisa Green

p. 136   Thierry Vezon   thierryvezon.com

p. 137   Alexey Sergeev   asergeev.com

p. 138   Tristan Brown   www.flickr.com/photos/tr1stan27

p. 139   Florent Dichy   www.flickr.com/photos/agilulfe

p. 140   ladylikebehavior.tumblr.com

p. 141   T. Mayne   animatedcatastrophe.deviantart.com

p. 142   fPat Murray   www.flickr.com/photos/fpat

p. 143   Jenna Lou Gorko   www.flickr.com/photos/justmejennalou

p. 144   Damian Steer   www.flickr.com/photos/pldms

p. 145   Celeste   www.flickr.com/photos/slowpokecelly

p. 146   Peter Firus/Flagstaffotos www.flagstaffotos.com.au

p. 147   Lisa Bingham

p. 148   Nick Taylor and Kim Mason   www.inckdesign.co.uk

p. 149   Rita Petita   www.flickr.com/photos/ritapetita

p. 150   Tambako the Jaguar   www.flickr.com/photos/tambako

p. 151   Stephen Oung   www.flickr.com/photos/stephen-oung

p. 152   Roderique Arisiaman   dracorubio.com

p. 153   Judit Pungor   www.flickr.com/photos/judt

p. 154   Nicholas Brown   www.flickr.com/photos/nsgbrown

p. 155   Glen (Shaggy) Roberts www.flickr.com/photos/51021547@N03

p. 156   Meredith Mahan

p. 157   Sam Howzit   www.flickr.com/photos/aloha75